AnglePlay™
BLOCKS

Simple Half-Rectangle Triangles, 84 No-Math Quilt Blocks, Easy-to-Follow Charts

MARGARET J. MILLER

C&T PUBLISHING

Text © 2005 Margaret Miller

Artwork © 2005 C&T Publishing, Inc.

Publisher: Amy Marson

Editorial Director: Gailen Runge

Acquisitions Editor: Jan Grigsby

Editor: Liz Aneloski

Technical Editor: Ellen Pahl

Copyeditor/Proofreader: Wordfirm Inc.

Cover Designer: Christina D. Jarumay

Design Director/Book Designer: Christina D. Jarumay

Illustrator: John Heisch

Production Assistants: Shawn Garcia and Tim Manibusan

Photography: Mark Frey, unless otherwise noted

Published by C&T Publishing, Inc., P.O. Box 1456, Lafayette, CA 94549

Front cover: *Batiks, etc.* by Margaret Miller

Back cover: *Untitled*, by Diana Johnston, *Is it Purple or Orange?*, by Pamela Thomas, *Cartwheel* by Cathy Hamilton

Library of Congress Cataloging-in-Publication Data

Miller, Margaret J.,

Angleplay : blocks : simple half-rectangle triangles, 84 no-math quilt blocks, easy-to-follow charts / Margaret Miller.

p. cm.

Includes bibliographical references.

ISBN 1-57120-294-3

1. Quilting—Patterns. 2. Geometrical drawing. I. Title: Angle play. II. Title.

TT835.M518 2005

746.46'041—dc22

2004028720

Printed in China

10 9 8 7 6 5 4 3 2 1

DEDICATION

To Linda N. Gunby: my guardian angel, my mentor, keeper of perspective, organizer of all necessary things, and most of all, my friend. Thank you, Linda!

ACKNOWLEDGMENTS

A thousand thank-yous to all who experimented with my AnglePlay™ templates and shared their results in record time! Thanks especially to those who shared their quilts for this book:

Karen Fettig Abramson, Poughkeepsie, NY

Kendra Allen, Poulsbo, WA

Nancy Anderson, Vancouver, WA

Cathy C. Bertrand, Nashville, TN

Teri Bever, Sedro Woolley, WA

Shelby Boyd, Franklin, TN

Jan Brown, Trinidad, CA

Elise Fare, Jacksonville, FL

Margaret Fourhman, Covington, WA

Beth Gardner, Midland, MI

Kathy Geehan, Bainbridge Island, WA

Cathy Hamilton, Arcata, CA

Patsi Hanseth, Mount Vernon, WA

Marilyn Hiestand, Hawaii National Park, HI

Mabel Huseby, Mount Vernon, WA

Diana Johnston, Snohomish, WA

Marty Kutz, Sedro Woolley, WA

Janet Lane-Tranbarger, Riverside, CA

Dixie McClain, Eden, ID

Faye Nutting, Sitka, AK

Reynola Pakusich, Bellingham, WA

Becky Poisson, Boulder Creek, CA

Barbara Powers, Yorktown Heights, NY

Beth Matsui Rice, Catonsville, MD

Maurine Roy, Edmonds, WA

Andrea Rudman, Kingston, WA

Pamela Thomas, Hayward, CA

Connie Tiegel, Atherton, CA

Thanks to Wanda Rains for her inspired and timely machine quilting, which added even more life to the quilts I took to her. Patsi Hanseth and Jennifer Pielow played a big part in the machine quilting of my works in this book as well. Thank you all.

And to Mark Frey, the photographer; thanks for showcasing my work so well over the years! To Diane Pederson at C&T Publishing, for overseeing the digital photography of the mock-ups and the how-to photographs; thanks for making this process so easy!

Most of all, heartfelt thanks to Liz Aneloski, my editor at C&T, and to all the staff at C&T Publishing; it is a delight to have you on my team!

CONTENTS

PREFACE

We quiltmakers love playing with shapes: We combine squares and half-square triangles to create a multitude of block designs. We can create an almost infinite number of blocks with these two shapes alone, using just two angles: 90° (the corner of a square) and 45° (the points of a right triangle).

But there is another shape, the half-rectangle triangle, that introduces numerous new angles to the patchwork palette. It breathes new life into the patchwork block designs we love so much. With the additional angles this shape provides, we can create the look of flowing and curved (even circular) lines across the patchwork surface, all with straight-line piecing.

The process of playing with this shape probably began the first time I "just for fun" drafted a traditional block into a rectangular, rather than a square, shape. This process transformed the shape of individual patches in the block and added numerous angles to the 90° and 45° angles that appear in traditional patchwork blocks. Thus, my motto, "Change the Angle," was born as a sure way to reach for the unexpected in the look of my quilts.

My fascination with the half-rectangle shape led to writing a book entitled *Blockbender Quilts*. In that book, I taught quilters how to make templates for these new angles. However, in this, my latest book, quiltmakers have a choice—make your own templates or purchase a set of acrylic AnglePlay™ templates, which I designed specifically for rotary cutting half-rectangle triangles to facilitate piecing this shape.

The half-rectangle triangle does appear in several traditional blocks. But until now, it has been a challenge to piece because of the excess seam allowance that extends beyond the most elongated point of the triangle. Quilters traditionally had to make templates and mark the seam intersections on the triangle ends. Then they had to carefully match the points and pin precisely before piecing.

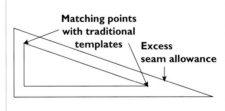

Matching points with traditional templates

Excess seam allowance

A simple experiment on graph paper will show the geometry conundrum this shape represents for quilters. Draw a square, add a ¼" seam allowance, and divide that square corner-to-corner (representing a pieced square). Note that the diagonal goes through the corners of the seamlines *and* the corners of the cutting lines. If you do the same with a rectangular shape to draw a pieced rectangle, note where the diagonal seamline exits the corners

of the cutting line. With every different size rectangle, the diagonal seam exits the cut edges at a different place.

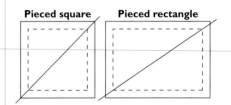

Pieced square   Pieced rectangle

The solution to the dilemmas of excess seam allowance, difficult matching, and the unpredictable emergence of the diagonal seam is a set of AnglePlay™ templates for rotary cutting the half-rectangle shapes. Each template, on which this book is based, is trimmed at exactly the correct angle, taking all the guesswork out of how two fabric triangles are matched up to be sewn. Moreover, the sewn results are accurate every time—the diagonal seam of the half-rectangle shape meets the corner of the finished block perfectly!

When I developed the AnglePlay™ templates and started testing them in classes and workshops throughout the summer of 2002, they met with universal acclaim! The more I explored the potential of this shape with workshop students and experimental groups, the more amazed I was at the world of possibilities these templates provide. This truly is *the next classic shape in patchwork* after squares and half-square triangles.

In perusing Barbara Brackman's *Encyclopedia of Pieced Quilt Patterns,* my student Teri Bever counted 44 traditional blocks that include the half-rectangle triangle shape. Marty Kutz used the AnglePlay™ templates to make one of these blocks, Nancy Cabot's Four Windmills, in her quilt *Northwest Winter*.

In addition to using the half-rectangle shape in traditional blocks, you can make various units and play with them as you might with wooden tangrams. This is what Diana Johnston did in her quilt shown below right. She made four large Nine-Patch blocks that feature not only traditional elements (half- and quarter-square triangles) but also half-rectangle triangles. By surrounding these blocks with a narrow border made exclusively of the latter shapes, she created a secondary star image in the center.

Another way to incorporate half-rectangle triangle shapes in a pieced quilt is to use both square and rectangular versions of a traditional block. A magnificent example of this is Becky Poisson's *Blooms A-Bloomin'* shown below.

This book does not include the traditional blocks mentioned here. Instead, it builds on that patchwork tradition. A few of the blocks in this book are reinterpretations of traditional blocks, but most are original blocks I developed by playing with colored paper shapes on my kitchen counter and photographing the results. My workshop students designed some of the blocks using the same process.

During my design process, so many blocks emerged that I had to stop myself from generating more of them—at block number 233! Eventually I used the computer program EQ5 to organize the blocks and to develop even more designs. Without EQ5, this book would still not be finished. Welcome to the wide, wide world of AnglePlay™!

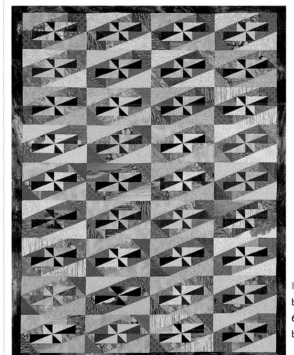

■ *Northwest Winter* by Marty Kutz, Sedro Woolley, WA, 62″ × 78″, 2004. Machine quilted by Patsi Hanseth.

■ *Blooms A-Bloomin'* by Becky Poisson, Boulder Creek, CA, 53″ × 53″, 2004.

■ *Untitled* by Diana Johnston, Snohomish, WA, 26½″ × 26½″, 2003.

INTRODUCTION

How to Use This Book

This is a reference book of pieced blocks that include the half-rectangle triangle as a key design element. I'm sure it will soon become one of the mainstays in your library of quiltmaking basics, and your list of favorite patchwork block patterns will expand immeasurably with this hitherto unexplored shape—destined to be *the next classic shape in American patchwork* design.

First, peruse the color photographs in Chapter 2: Gallery of Blocks (pages 12–19) to see which blocks strike your fancy. Next, look at the blocks presented in gray-scale diagrams in Chapter 3: Block Patterns (pages 20–45) to see which blocks catch your attention; they may or may not be the same ones you liked in the color photographs! Chapter 3 provides all the information you need to make a block, including the specific templates needed and the number and size of shapes to cut to make 12″ blocks.

AnglePlay™ Templates

If you have a set of AnglePlay™ templates, you are all set to choose your fabrics and start cutting. If not, you can make your own templates using the patterns in Appendix A (pages 58–62). Refer to Making Your Own Templates at right for further details. See Resources (page 64) for information on purchasing a set of acrylic AnglePlay™ templates designed to use with your rotary cutter.

Look through Chapter 4: Blocks to Quilts (pages 46–51) to get inspiration for making your first AnglePlay quilt. And, of course, there is Chapter 5: Gallery of Quilts (pages 52–57) to really set your creativity spinning. Many of these quilts were made by students who were in my experimental classes and in the first AnglePlay workshops. It's always a delight for a teacher to see students run in so many wonderful directions with a new idea! For even more ideas, see my book *Smashing Sets: Innovative Settings for Sampler Blocks.* Use the plans in that book and substitute AnglePlay blocks.

Supplies

In addition to the templates, you will need only the basic sewing and quilting supplies. But read on for some helpful information regarding supplies for AnglePlay quilts.

FABRICS

Use good-quality, high-thread-count fabrics. You will be cutting across the grain of the fabric at many bias angles, and a fabric with a higher thread count will mean less distortion and stretch.

ROTARY CUTTING EQUIPMENT

Use a rotary cutter with a sharp blade (to save wear and tear on your wrists and fingers). Since you must cut four sides of the template to create this shape, use a small cutting mat that you can rotate. That way you can cut one or two sides of the template and then rotate the cutting mat as needed. You will not have to disturb the positioning of the template on the fabric to make the remaining cuts.

PINS

Use silk pins rather than standard straight pins for pinning and matching block pieces. These pins are fine and thin, are easier to use, and distort the bias edge less. I like the silk pins with a round glass head for easy retrieval.

Making Your Own Templates

If you choose to use the patterns in Appendix A (pages 58–62) to create your own templates, use the sturdiest (thickest) transparent template plastic your quilt shop has to offer. Clear template plastic is easier for this process than plastic with a grid printed on it. Be sure to trace and cut the templates *very* carefully. Of course, to create your block in fabric, you will have the added step of tracing around your plastic template before cutting it out. You can still cut several layers of fabric at a time, but be sure that you trace the shape carefully and accurately.

TEMPLATE RACKS

I strongly recommend that you store your templates standing upright in a slotted stand or rack on your worktable. That way, the templates will be readily accessible and easy to organize. Template racks are available through your local quilt shop or from the source listed in Resources (page 64).

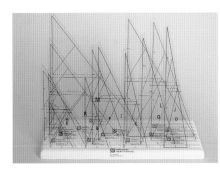

Guide to Cutting

These instructions assume that you are using the commercially available acrylic templates. With these, you can cut around the shape with a rotary cutter. Or you can use a rotary cutter and small rotary ruler to cut multiple layers along the lines after drawing around your template onto the fabric. Do not try to cut through more than six layers of fabric.

Layer your fabrics so that the right side of each is facing up. Position the template on the fabric so the straight of the grain will run along the straight edges of the template. That way, the resulting pieced rectangle will have straight grain edges. The diagonal seam should be the only one that is on the bias, unless you are using a directional print or stripe, which would require you to position the template otherwise.

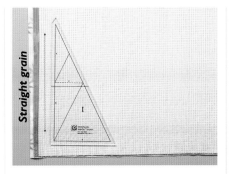

tip EASY CUTTING

When cutting around the template, move to a different side of your cutting table, or rotate the mat as needed.

Note that there are right-facing and left-facing triangles. The block you choose will dictate which one you cut. Always cut with your fabrics right side up, and flip the template to the reverse side as necessary. There is an exception to this rule: If you are making a directional block, cutting triangles from fabrics that are both right side up and wrong side up can create blocks that appear to spin in opposite directions. See Block Variations (pages 43–44) for further information.

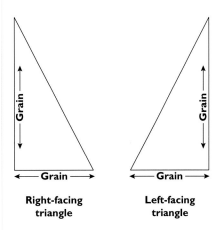

Right-facing triangle   **Left-facing triangle**

tip TRIANGLES WANTED

Don't worry if you happen to cut extra triangles for any block or quilt. I love these! They're like a sourdough starter…all ready to begin the next quilt!

CUTTING FULL-SIZE ANGLEPLAY SHAPES

On each AnglePlay™ template, there are two sizes of triangles—full-size and half-size.

To cut several of the same full-size triangles from a given fabric or set of fabrics, cut a strip of each fabric, slightly wider than the template you will be using.

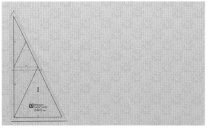

If cutting only a single shape from a large piece of fabric, position the template near a corner of the fabric. Make the first two cuts so that you can move the bulk of the fabric away from the cut area. Then rotate the cutting mat to make the third cut along the remaining side of the triangle and the fourth short cut at the point.

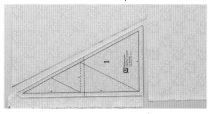

CUTTING HALF-SIZE ANGLEPLAY SHAPES

In the patterns in Chapter 3, the smaller half-size triangle on each template is noted with the number 1 after the template letter. For example, if the cutting for a block calls for I1, that would be the half-triangle for Template I.

1. To cut the half-size shape, place the appropriate template near the corner of the fabric. Make a straightening cut using the template's right-angle corner. Be sure to cut beyond the halfway line on the long side of the triangle.

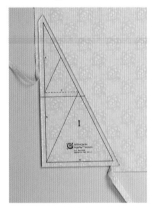

2. Slide the template so that one cut edge of the fabric aligns with the baseline of the smaller half-rectangle triangle. Align the straight edge of the template with the other cut edge of the fabric.

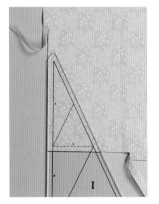

3. Cut along the diagonal edge and along the tip of the triangle.

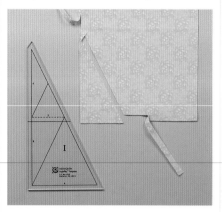

MAKING PIECED TRIANGLES

Each template has a diagonal line that cuts the triangle in half, from the straight-grain corner to the midpoint of the opposite edge. I call this the "half-diagonal line." With this line, you can create a pieced triangle that will greatly expand the number of blocks and designs you can make. This gives you a much more complex looking design from simple shapes, often creating a three-dimensional look on the two-dimensional surface.

To create the pieced triangle, you will rough cut the half-triangle pieces first, sew them together, and then cut with your template. Select the appropriate AnglePlay™ template and follow the instructions below.

Note that the longer, narrower triangle is labeled "A," and the other triangle is labeled "B." The seam that joins them is called the half-diagonal.

CUTTING SECTION A

1. Place the template on the fabric so the fabric's straight grain is along the triangle's longest edge. Position the template at least 1/2″ from the fabric edges.

2. Beginning about 2/3 of the way down from the tip of the triangle, cut along the diagonal (bias edge).

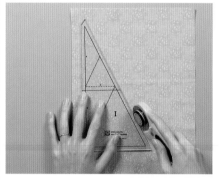

3. Fold back the cut edge of the fabric and turn the template over. Reposition the template so the longest edge is still on the straight grain 1/2″ from the fabric's edge and so the template's half-diagonal line is parallel to and at least 1/2″ from the fabric edge you just cut. Cut along the diagonal (bias edge). Cut beyond the point of the template, all the way to the raw edge of the fabric. Place the shape on the design wall or set aside.

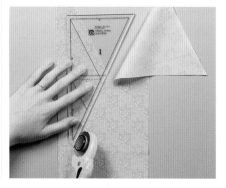

CUTTING SECTION B

1. Place the template on the fabric so the triangle's base is on the fabric's straight grain. Position the template at least ½″ from the fabric edges.

2. Proceed as you did for cutting A. Cut along the diagonal, beginning about ⅔ of the way down the template from the raw edge at the top. Cut along the diagonal to the top raw edge.

3. Fold back the cut edge of the fabric so it is out of the way. Rotate the cutting mat 180°. Flip the template over, placing the straight-grain edge ½″ from the raw edge and the half-diagonal line on the template ½″ from and parallel to the edge you just cut. Cut along the diagonal, and place next to section A.

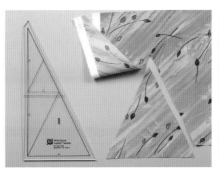

JOINING SECTIONS A AND B

Note that A and B are rough cut considerably larger than what you need. Therefore, you don't have to worry about careful alignment of the A and B pieces. You will trim the edges later.

1. Align the A and B pieces along the half-diagonal seam. Sew the pieces together using a ¼″ seam allowance. Press the seam open.

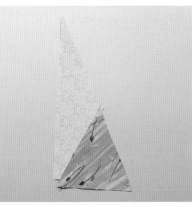

2. Reposition the template on the joined fabrics, aligning the half-diagonal line on the template with the sewn seam. Rotary cut around the template. Place on the design wall.

CUTTING OTHER SHAPES

The pieced rectangles that you make from the triangles are used in the blocks along with squares, pieced squares, and rectangles. Cut the needed shapes with your rotary cutter and regular rotary-cutting rulers. Each block pattern lists the sizes to cut.

Squares: Cut a square of fabric ½″ larger than the desired finished size.

Half-square triangles: Cut a square of fabric ⅞″ larger than the desired finished size. Cut corner-to-corner once. Sew appropriate triangles.

Quarter-square triangles: Cut a square of fabric 1¼″ larger than the desired finished size. Cut corner-to-corner both ways. Sew appropriate triangles together.

Rectangles: Cut a rectangle of fabric ½″ larger than desired finished size.

Triangle Piecing Tips

First, you need to make certain that your seam allowance will be accurate. Take a template to the sewing machine and place it under the presser foot. Lower the needle so it touches the template's seamline. Notice where the edge of the template falls on your machine's throat plate; this is where the raw edge of your triangles should be as you sew them together. *This may or may not be what you currently use as your 1/4″ seam guide.*

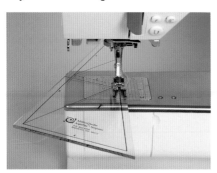

Sew all the diagonal seams first. Then, join the resulting rectangles and any other patches into rows or into larger pieced units, according to the block instructions. Press all seams open; this distributes the bulk of seam allowances as evenly as possible, regardless of the angle of the seams coming together when joining blocks and units.

Since you are beginning your seam at the point of the triangles, be sure to hold both threads (top and bobbin) taut behind the presser foot as you take your first stitches. This will keep the beginning of your seam from "disappearing" down through your machine's throat plate, making an annoying mess!

PIECING ACCURACY

The templates are designed so that you will be able to line up two triangles quickly and easily, using the angle you cut at the narrow point. It works like a dream. You don't even have to mark any dots for the seam allowances. Pin the patches before sewing—careful pinning helps yield precise piecing. Stitch a 1/4″ seam along the diagonal, and press the seam open.

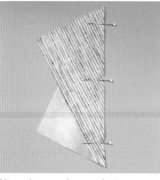

Align the patches and pin.

tip
NO TRIMMING NEEDED
There's no need to trim the dog-ears. By pretrimming the elongated point of the half-rectangle triangle with the AnglePlay™ templates, you have already reduced the bulk where seams will intersect.

After sewing your first seam, check to be sure that the diagonal seam is going to hit the corner properly. To do this, on a sheet of graph paper, draw the finished size of the rectangle you are making and add the 1/4″ seam allowance all around. Draw the diagonal of the *finished* size rectangle from

corner to corner, and extend it out beyond the outer rectangle.

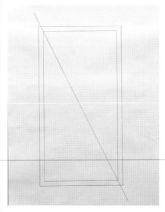

Place your sewn and pressed rectangle unit onto your graph paper drawing. If the two corners of the paper model don't align with the seam you just sewed, recheck the seam allowance you used against a template to make sure that you are *sewing* the same seam allowance that you *cut* with the AnglePlay™ templates.

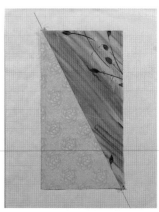

Right

Wrong

When joining rows or larger units of pieced rectangles, place the units to be joined right sides together, and place a pin through the precise points that you want to meet at the seam. Leave that pin perpendicular to the fabric. Pin normally on each side of the perpendicular pin. Pin the rest of the seam in preparation for sewing.

Leave the perpendicular pin in place until you can't sew any further without removing it.

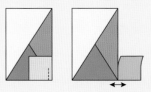

With this method, your seamlines will meet precisely, and you will have nice sharp points.

Working with the half-rectangle shape and the AnglePlay™ templates will help you develop your sense of precision and craftsmanship in sewing patchwork blocks and quilts. You will improve your piecing skills, almost in spite of yourself!

■ PARTIAL SEAM CONSTRUCTION

Several of the blocks in this book use partial seam construction. This technique creates blocks that look complex but are easy to sew by following the steps below. Most of the blocks of this type have a square unit in the center, with rectangular or square units around it. The center square can be a single patch or a pieced unit. Here are two examples of blocks that require partial seams.

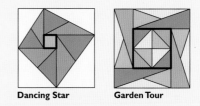

Dancing Star   Garden Tour

1. With right sides together, align the center square with the adjacent rectangular unit. Sew the square about halfway across, or stop stitching 1" from the edge, leaving the remainder of the piece free. Press.

2. Align the next unit, right sides together, and stitch the second seam. Work your way around the block, adding each unit in order. Then complete the partial seam between the final unit and the first unit. Press.

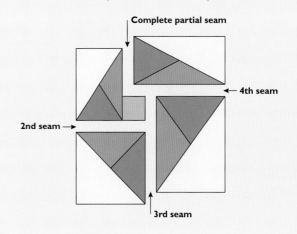

Complete partial seam

4th seam

2nd seam →

3rd seam

2

GALLERY
OF BLOCKS

With each block, we have listed its name and the page where the gray-scale block diagram and piecing diagram appear. The gray-scale version of the block includes light, medium, and dark values. In many cases, the value placements in the gray-scale illustration are different from the colored version in this chapter. This shows you how the same block can look very different, depending on placement of values.

Double Star (page 21)

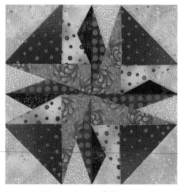

Janet's Fancy (page 21)

Buttercup Glory (page 22)

Christmas Star (page 21)

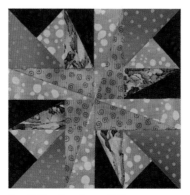

Deal 'Em Out (page 21)

Barbed Wire (page 22)

Periscope (page 22)

Turkey Cheeks (page 23)

Barnacles (page 24)

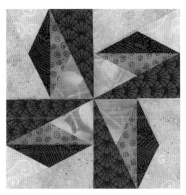

Comin' Home (page 22)

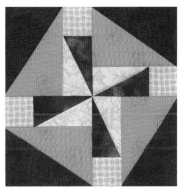

Control Tower (page 23)

Ann's Plans (page 24)

Origami Star (page 23)

Twisted (page 24)

Organ Grinder (page 25)

Candy Jar (page 23)

Scout's Star (page 24)

Cricket (page 25)

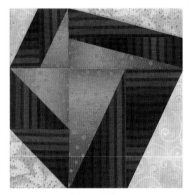

Four Winds (page 25)

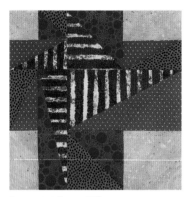

Pony Tail (page 26)

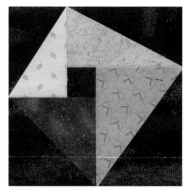

Treasure Box (page 27)

North Star (page 25)

French Twist (page 26)

Dancing Star (page 28)

Whirlwind (page 26)

Pam's Folly (page 27)

Beribboned (page 28)

In the Swing of Things (page 26)

Twinkle, Twinkle (page 27)

Garden Tour (page 28)

Spiderweb (page 28)

Delicate Balance (page 29)

Eye of the Storm (page 30)

Polliwog (page 29)

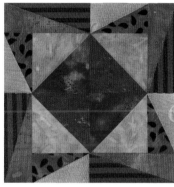

Harlequin (page 30)

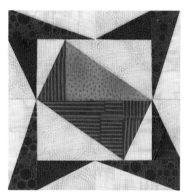

Special Delivery (page 31)

Twist Tie (page 29)

Mapped Out (page 30)

Christmas Cactus (page 31)

Square Dance (page 29)

Tiger Lily (page 30)

Folded Fern (page 31)

Bread Box (page 31)

Jack in the Pulpit (page 33)

Daisy, Daisy (page 34)

Hide and Seek (page 32)

Leaves of Grass (page 33)

Crab Cakes (page 34)

Canasta (page 32)

Pretty Posey (page 33)

Hydrangea (page 35)

Nosegay (page 32)

Morning Glory (page 34)

Palm Frond (page 35)

Bee's Knees (page 35)

Lightning Bug (page 36)

Four Leaf Clover (page 37)

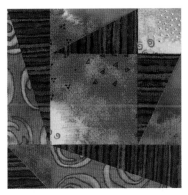
Baby Birds (page 35)

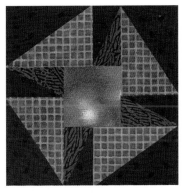
Tiger Eye (page 36)

Orangeade (page 37)

Agate Pass (page 36)

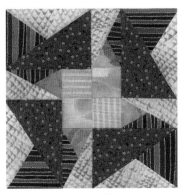
Joyful Noise (page 37)

Shooting Star (page 38)

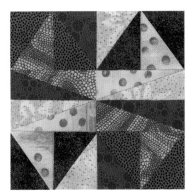
Taffy Pull (page 36)

First Star (page 37)

Salisbury (page 38)

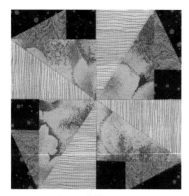

Hancock (page 38)

Pembroke (page 39)

Headed Home (page 40)

Mad Hatter (page 38)

Park Place (page 39)

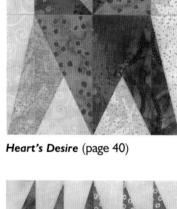

Heart's Desire (page 40)

Keep Right (page 39)

Noonday Sun (page 39)

March of the Diamonds (page 40)

All Shook Up (page 40)

Tornado (page 41)

Carousel (page 42)

Tilted Windmill (page 41)

Braided Bounds (page 41)

Moonglow (page 42)

Spiral Staircase (page 41)

Siesta (page 42)

Chuggin' Along (page 42)

3

BLOCK PATTERNS

This chapter holds all the information you need to make the AnglePlay blocks presented in Chapter 2, plus many more! At the end of this chapter, I've included several ways of varying these blocks to come up with versions of your own.

How to Read the Diagrams

Each block is first presented in a gray-scale shaded diagram. Included with each block diagram are the dimensions of the units within the block. The templates and cutting instructions for all the blocks will yield a 12″ block.

The second illustration is an unshaded piecing diagram, with a number for each different patch. The chart lists the patch numbers and how many to cut of each. The letters in the chart refer to the letters on the template patterns in Appendix A (pages 58–62) and correspond to the letters on the AnglePlay™ templates. When a template letter has the number 1 after it, cut the half-size triangle in the upper portion of the template.

I have kept the cutting charts as simple as possible to give you freedom to vary the values and value placement. This gives you many different looks for any individual block. For example, when the cutting chart indicates that for Patches 3–6 you are to cut "2 ea: B," this means you need to cut two of Template B for each Patch 3–6, for a total of 8 patches. You need to determine how many B patches of

each value or color to cut. Choose fabric colors and values carefully to achieve the necessary contrast.

The icons in the charts represent the shape you will be cutting. When the icons are divided along the half-diagonal, you will need to rough cut the shapes first and then piece them. Refer to Making Pieced Triangles (Chapter 1, pages 8–9) for details.

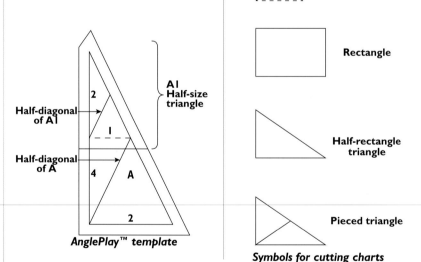

AnglePlay™ template

Symbols for cutting charts

Square

Half-square triangle

Quarter-square triangle

Rectangle

Half-rectangle triangle

Pieced triangle

> *tip* **DOWNSIZING**
>
> *If a block is very simple with few pieces, such as Twinkle, Twinkle (page 27), you can create a 6″ block by using the smaller (half-size) triangles on the listed templates. For more complex blocks, such as Daisy, Daisy (page 34), I recommend foundation piecing if you want to make a 6″ block. In this case, draft the 6″ block on paper, divide it into units as shown in the piecing diagram, and copy onto your preferred foundation.*

The Blocks

DOUBLE STAR

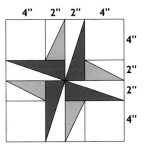

Templates: **A, B;** Color photo on page 12.

PATCH	CUT
I	4: 4½″
2, 3	4 ea: A
4, 5	4 ea: B

CHRISTMAS STAR

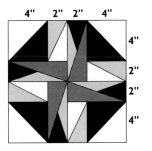

Templates: **A, B;** Color photo on page 12.

PATCH	CUT	SUBCUT
1, 2	2 ea: 4⅞″	4 ea:
3, 4	4 ea: A	
5	4: B	
6	4: B	

JANET'S FANCY

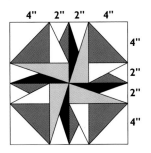

Templates: **A, B;** Color photo on page 12.

PATCH	CUT	SUBCUT
1, 2	2 ea: 4⅞″	4 ea:
3	4: A	
4	4: A	
5	4: B	
6	4: B	

DEAL 'EM OUT

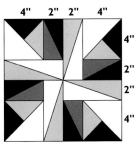

Templates: **A, B;** Color photo on page 12.

PATCH	CUT	SUBCUT
I	2: 4⅞″	4:
2, 3	I ea: 5¼″	4 ea:
4, 5	4 ea: A	
6, 7	4 ea: B	

BUTTERCUP GLORY

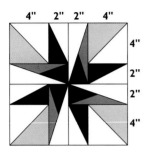

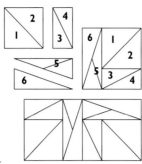

PATCH	CUT	SUBCUT
1, 2	2 ea: $4\frac{7}{8}''$	4 ea:
3, 4	4 ea: A	
5	4: B	
6	4: B	

Templates: A, B; Color photo on page 12.

BARBED WIRE

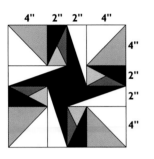

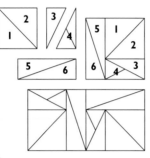

PATCH	CUT	SUBCUT
1, 2	2 ea: $4\frac{7}{8}''$	4 ea:
3	4: A	
4	4: A	
5, 6	4 ea: B	

Templates: A, B; Color photo on page 12.

PERISCOPE

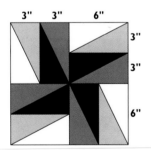

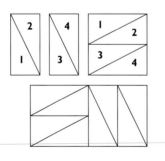

PATCH	CUT
1, 2, 3, 4	4 ea: E

Template: E; Color photo on page 13.

COMIN' HOME

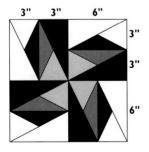

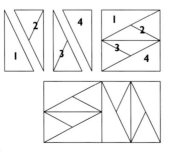

PATCH	CUT
1, 4	4 ea: E
2, 3	4 ea: E

Template: E; Color photo on page 13.

ORIGAMI STAR

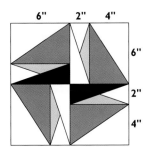

6" 2" 4" | 6" 2" 4"

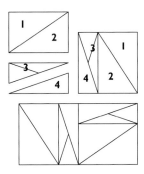

PATCH	CUT
1, 2	4 ea: H
3	4: B
4	4: B

Templates: B, H; Color photo on page 13.

CANDY JAR

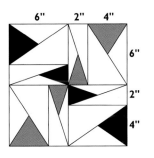

6" 2" 4" | 6" 2" 4"

PATCH	CUT	
1	4: H	◁
2	4: H	◹
3	4: B	
4	4: B	◁

Templates: B, H; Color photo on page 13.

TURKEY CHEEKS

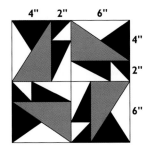

4" 2" 6" | 4" 2" 6"

PATCH	CUT	SUBCUT
1	4: H ◺	
2	4: H	
3, 4	2 ea: 2⅞"	4 ea:
5, 6	4 ea: A	

Templates: A, H; Color photo on page 13.

CONTROL TOWER

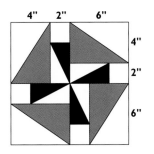

4" 2" 6" | 4" 2" 6"

PATCH	CUT	
1, 2	4 ea: H	◺
3	4: 2½"	
4, 5	4 ea: A	

Templates: A, H; Color photo on page 13.

TWISTED

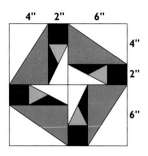

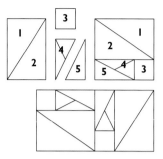

PATCH	CUT
1, 2	4 ea: H
3	4: 2½″
4	4: A
5	4: A

Templates: A, H; Color photo on page 13.

SCOUT'S STAR

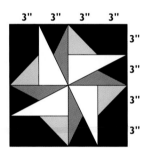

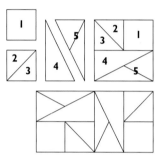

PATCH	CUT	SUBCUT
1	4: 3½″	
2, 3	2 ea: 3⅞″	4 ea:
4	4: E	
5	4: E	

Template: E; Color photo on page 13.

BARNACLES

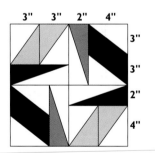

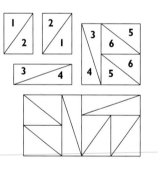

PATCH	CUT
1, 2, 5, 6	4 ea: K1
3, 4	4 ea: B

Templates: B, K1; Color photo on page 13.

ANN'S PLANS

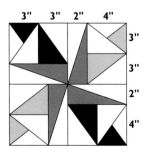

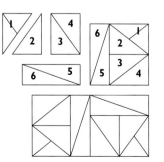

PATCH	CUT	
1	4: K1	◺
2	4: K1	◹
3, 4	4 ea: K1	◿
5, 6	4 ea: B	

Templates: B, K1; Color photo on page 13.

ORGAN GRINDER

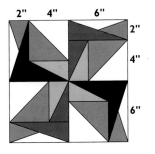

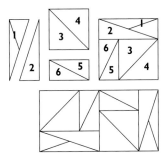

PATCH	CUT	SUBCUT
1	4: B	
2	4: B	
3, 4	2 ea: $4\frac{7}{8}''$	4 ea:
5, 6	4 ea: A	

Templates: A, B; Color photo on page 13.

CRICKET

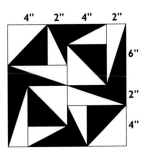

PATCH	CUT	SUBCUT
1, 2	2 ea: $4\frac{7}{8}''$	4 ea:
3, 4	4 ea: A	
5, 6	4 ea: B	

Templates: A, B; Color photo on page 13.

FOUR WINDS

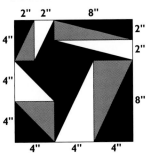

PATCH	CUT	SUBCUT
1–4	1 ea: A	
5–8	1 ea: C	
9–12	1 ea: I	
13–16	1 ea: $4\frac{7}{8}''$	1 ea:

Templates: A, C, I; Color photo on page 14.

NORTH STAR

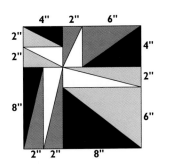

PATCH	CUT
1–6	1 ea: A
7, 8	1 ea: H
9, 10, 13, 14, 15, 16	1 ea: C
11, 12	1 ea: K

Templates: A, C, H, K; Color photo on page 14.

WHIRLWIND

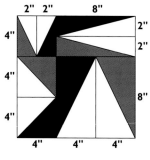
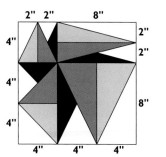

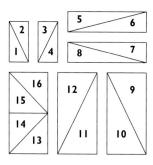

PATCH	CUT	SUBCUT
1, 2	1 ea: A	
3, 4	1 ea: A	
5, 6	1 ea: C	
7, 8	1 ea: C	
9, 10	1 ea: I	
11, 12	1 ea: I	
13–16	1 ea: 4⅞″	1 ea:

Templates: A, C, I; Color photo on page 14.

IN THE SWING OF THINGS

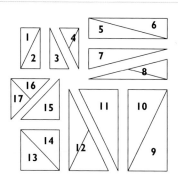

PATCH	CUT	SUBCUT
1, 2	1 ea: A	
3	1: A	
4	1: A	
5, 6	1 ea: C	
7	1: C	
8	1: C	
9, 10	1 ea: I	
11	1: I	
12	1: I	
13–15	1 ea: 4⅞″	1 ea:
16, 17	1 ea: 5¼″	1 ea:

Templates: A, C, I; Color photo on page 14.

PONY TAIL

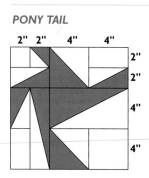
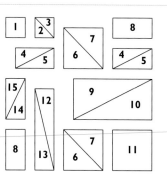

PATCH	CUT	SUBCUT
1	1: 2½″	
2, 3	1 ea: 2⅞″	1 ea:
4, 5	2 ea: A	
6, 7	1 ea: 4⅞″	2 ea:
8	2: 2½″ x 4½″	
9, 10	1 ea: I	
11	1: 4½″	
12, 13	1 ea: C	
14, 15	1 ea: A	

Templates: A, C, I; Color photo on page 14.

FRENCH TWIST

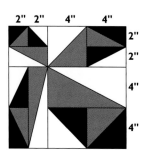
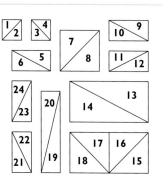

PATCH	CUT	SUBCUT
1–4	1 ea: 2⅞″	1 ea:
5, 6, 9, 10 23, 24	1 ea: A	
7, 8, 15–18	1 ea: 4⅞″	1 ea:
11, 12, 21, 22	1 ea: A	
13, 14	1 ea: I	
19, 20	1 ea: C	

Templates: A, C, I; Color photo on page 14.

PAM'S FOLLY

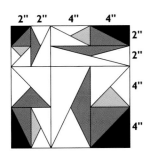

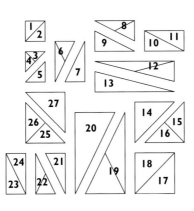

Templates: A, C, I
Color photo on page 14.

PATCH	CUT	SUBCUT
1, 2, 5	1 ea: $2\frac{7}{8}''$	1 ea:
3, 4	1 ea: $3\frac{1}{4}''$	1 ea:
6, 8	1 ea: A	
7, 9, 10, 11	1 ea: A	
12	1: C	
13	1: C	
14, 17, 18, 27	1 ea: $4\frac{7}{8}''$	1 ea:
15, 16, 25, 26	1 ea: $5\frac{1}{4}''$	1 ea:
19	1: I	
20	1: I	
21, 23, 24	1 ea: A	
22	1: A	

TWINKLE, TWINKLE

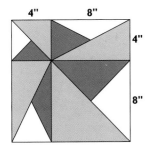

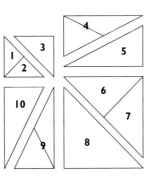

Template: I; Color photo on page 14.

PATCH	CUT	SUBCUT
1, 2	1 ea: $5\frac{1}{4}''$	1 ea:
3	1: $4\frac{7}{8}''$	1:
4	1: I	
5	1: I	
6, 7	1 ea: $9\frac{1}{4}''$	1 ea:
8	1: $8\frac{7}{8}''$	1:
9	1: I	
10	1: I	

TREASURE BOX

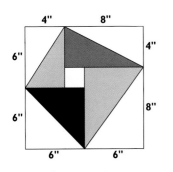

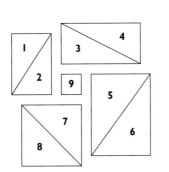

Templates: H, I, K
Color photo on page 14.

Note: *Sew this block together with a partial seam. See Partial Seam Construction (Chapter 1, page 11).*

PATCH	CUT	SUBCUT
1, 2	1 ea: H	
3, 4	1 ea: I	
5, 6	1 ea: K	
7, 8	1 ea: $6\frac{7}{8}''$	1 ea:
9	1: $2\frac{1}{2}''$	

DANCING STAR

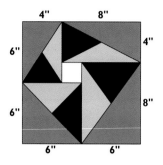

4" 8"
4"
6"
6"
6" 8"
6" 6"

Templates: H, I, K
Color photo on page 14.

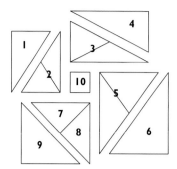

Note: Sew this block together with a partial seam. See Partial Seam Construction (Chapter 1, page 11).

PATCH	CUT	SUBCUT
I	I: H	
2	I: H	
3	I: I	
4	I: I	
5	I: K	
6	I: K	
7, 8	I ea: 7¼″	I ea:
9	I: 6⅞″	I:
10	I: 2½″	

BERIBBONED

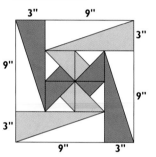

3" 9"
3"
9"
9"
3"
9" 3"

Template: G; Color photo on page 14.

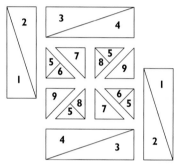

PATCH	CUT	SUBCUT
I–4	2 ea: G	
5	I: 4¼″	4:
6, 8	I ea: 4¼″	2 ea:
7, 9	I ea: 3⅞″	2 ea:

Note: Sew this block together with a partial seam. See Partial Seam Construction (Chapter 1, page 11).

GARDEN TOUR

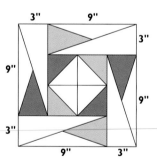

3" 9"
3"
9"
9"
3"
9" 3"

Template: G; Color photo on page 14.

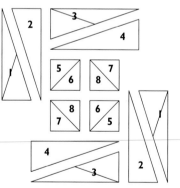

PATCH	CUT	SUBCUT
I, 3	2 ea: G	
2, 4	2 ea: G	
5–8	I ea: 3⅞″	2 ea:

Note: Sew this block together with a partial seam. See Partial Seam Construction (Chapter 1, page 11).

SPIDERWEB

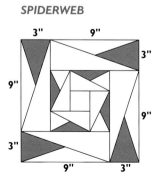

3" 9"
3"
9"
9"
3"
9" 3"

Templates: A, G; Color photo on page 15.

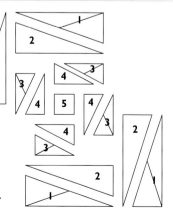

PATCH	CUT
I	4: G
2	4: G
3	4: A
4	4: A
5	I: 2½″

Note: Sew this block together with a partial seam. See Partial Seam Construction (Chapter 1, page 11).

POLLIWOG

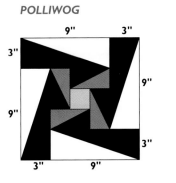

Templates: A, G; Color photo on page 15.

PATCH	CUT	
1, 2	4 ea: G	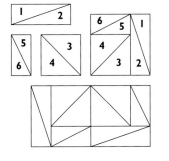
3, 4	4 ea: A	
5	1: 2½″	

Note: Sew this block together with a partial seam.
See Partial Seam Construction (Chapter 1, page 11).

TWIST TIE

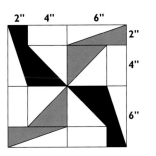

Template: B; Color photo on page 15.

PATCH	CUT	SUBCUT
1, 2	4 ea: B	
3	4: 2½″ x 4½″	
4, 5	2 ea: 4⅞″	4 ea:

SQUARE DANCE

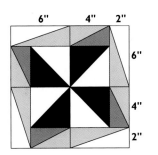

Templates: A, B; Color photo on page 15.

PATCH	CUT	SUBCUT
1, 2	4 ea: B	
3, 4	2 ea: 4⅞″	4 ea:
5, 6	4 ea: A	

DELICATE BALANCE

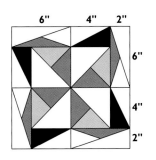

Templates: A, B; Color photo on page 15.

PATCH	CUT	SUBCUT
1	4: B	
2	4: B	
3, 4	1 ea: 5¼″	4 ea:
5	2: 4⅞″	4:
6, 7	4 ea: A	

HARLEQUIN

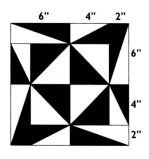

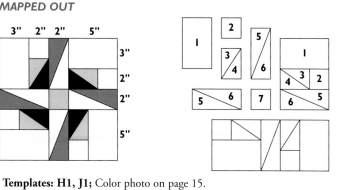

PATCH	CUT	SUBCUT
1, 2	4 ea: B	
3, 4	2 ea: $4^7/8''$	4 ea:
5, 6	4 ea: A	

Templates: A, B; Color photo on page 15.

MAPPED OUT

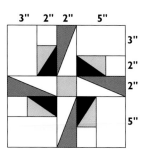

PATCH	CUT
1	4: $3^1/2'' \times 5^1/2''$
2	4: $2^1/2''$
3, 4	4 ea: H1
5, 6	4 ea: J1
7	1: $2^1/2''$

Templates: H1, J1; Color photo on page 15.

TIGER LILY

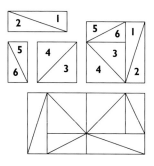

PATCH	CUT	SUBCUT
1, 2	4 ea: J1	
3, 4	4 ea: H1	
5, 6	4 ea: J1	
7, 8	2 ea: $3^7/8''$	4 ea:
9	1: $2^1/2''$	

Templates: H1, J1; Color photo on page 15.

EYE OF THE STORM

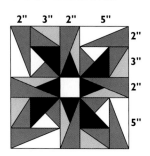

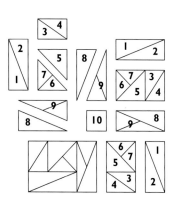

PATCH	CUT	SUBCUT
1, 2	4 ea: J1	
3, 4	4 ea: H1	
5	2: $3^7/8''$	4:
6, 7	1 ea: $4^1/4''$	4 ea:
8	4: J1	
9	4: J1	
10	1: $2^1/2''$	

Templates: H1, J1
Color photo on page 15.

SPECIAL DELIVERY

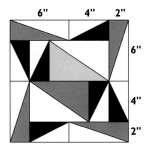

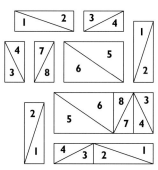

PATCH	CUT
1, 2	4 ea: B
3, 4	4 ea: A
5, 6	2 ea: H
7, 8	2 ea: A

Templates: A, B, H; Color photo on page 15.

CHRISTMAS CACTUS

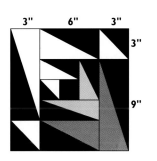

PATCH	CUT	SUBCUT
1, 2	2 ea: G	
3, 4	1 ea: 3⁷/₈″	2 ea:
5, 6	2 ea: E	
7, 8	1 ea: A	
9, 10	1 ea: 2⁷/₈″	1 ea:
11	1: 2¹/₂″	
12, 13	1 ea: B	
14, 15	1 ea: A	

Templates: A, B, E, G; Color photo on page 15.

FOLDED FERN

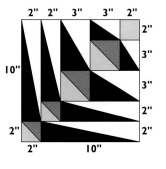

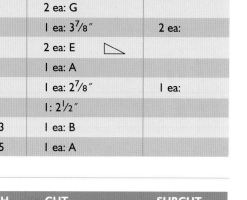

PATCH	CUT	SUBCUT
1	1: 2¹/₂″	
2, 3	1 ea: H1	
4, 5	1 ea: H1	
6, 7	1 ea: L1	
8, 9	1 ea: L1	
10, 11	1 ea: C	
12, 13	1 ea: C	
14, 15	1 ea: D	
16, 17	1 ea: D	
18, 19	1 ea: 2⁷/₈″	2 ea:
20, 21	1 ea: 3⁷/₈″	2 ea:

Templates: C, D, H1, L1
Color photo on page 15.

BREAD BOX

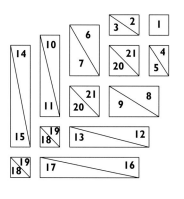

PATCH	CUT
1, 2	2 ea: J
3, 4	2 ea: C
5	1: I
6	1: I

Templates: C, J, I; Color photo on page 16.

HIDE AND SEEK

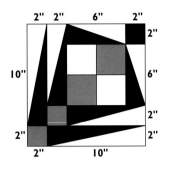

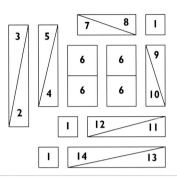

Templates: B, C, D
Color photo on page 16.

PATCH	CUT
I	3: 2 1/2"
2, 3	I ea: D
4, 5	I ea: C
6	4: 3 1/2"
7, 8	I ea: B
9, 10	I ea: B
II, 12	I ea: C
13, 14	I ea: D

CANASTA

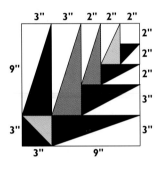

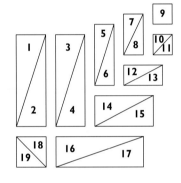

Templates: A, B, E, G
Color photo on page 16.

PATCH	CUT	SUBCUT
I–4	I ea: G	
5, 6	I ea: B	
7, 8	I ea: A	
9	I: 2 1/2"	
10, 11	I ea: 2 7/8"	I ea:
12, 13	I ea: A	
14, 15	I ea: E	
16, 17	I ea: G	
18, 19	I ea: 3 7/8"	I ea:

NOSEGAY

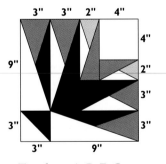

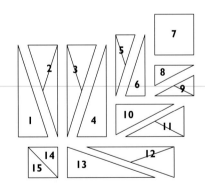

Templates: A, B, E, G
Color photo on page 16.

PATCH	CUT	SUBCUT
I	I: G	
2	I: G	
3, 12	I ea: G	
4, 13	I ea: G	
5	I: B	
6	I: B	
7	I: 4 1/2"	
8	I: A	
9	I: A	
10	I: E	
II	I: E	
14, 15	I ea: 3 7/8"	I ea:

JACK IN THE PULPIT

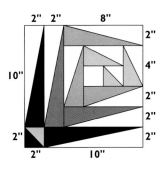

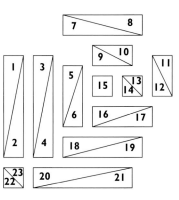

Templates: A, B, C, D
Color photo on page 16.

PATCH	CUT	SUBCUT
1–4	1 ea: D	
5, 6	1 ea: B	
7, 8	1 ea: C	
9, 10	1 ea: A	
11, 12	1 ea: A	
13, 14, 22, 23	1 ea: 2⁷⁄₈″	1 ea:
15	1: 2¹⁄₂″	
16, 17	1 ea: B	
18, 19	1 ea: C	
20, 21	1 ea: D	

LEAVES OF GRASS

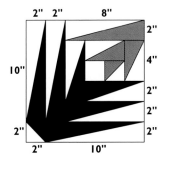

Templates: A, B, C, D
Color photo on page 16.

PATCH	CUT	SUBCUT
1, 2	2 ea: D	
3, 4	1 ea: B	
5, 6, 16, 17	1 ea: C	
7, 8	1 ea: A	
9, 10	1 ea: A	
11, 12, 20, 21	1 ea: 2⁷⁄₈″	1 ea:
13	1: 2¹⁄₂″	
14, 15	1 ea: B	
18, 19	1 ea: D	

PRETTY POSEY

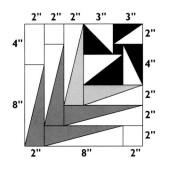

Templates: A, B, C, H1, K1
Color photo on page 16.

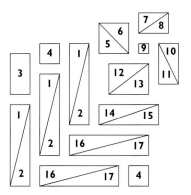

Note: Sew the unit in the upper right corner of this block with a partial seam. See Partial Seam Construction (Chapter 1, page 11).

PATCH	CUT	SUBCUT
1, 2	3 ea: C	
3	1: 2¹⁄₂″ x 4¹⁄₂″	
4	2: 2¹⁄₂″	
5, 6	1 ea: 3⁷⁄₈″	1 ea:
7, 8	1 ea: H1	
9	1: 1¹⁄₂″	
10, 11	1 ea: A	
12, 13	1 ea: K1	
14, 15	1 ea: B	
16, 17	2 ea: C	

MORNING GLORY

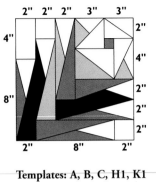

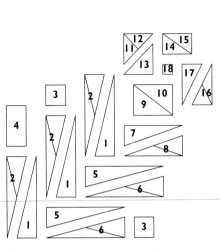

Templates: A, B, C, H1, K1
Color photo on page 16.

Note: *Sew the unit in the upper right corner of this block with a partial seam. See Partial Seam Construction (Chapter 1, page 11).*

PATCH	CUT	SUBCUT
1	3: C	
2	3: C	
3	2: 2½″	
4	1: 2½″ x 4½″	
5	2: C	
6	2: C	
7	1: B	
8	1: B	
9, 10	1 ea: K1	
11, 12	1 ea: 4¼″	1 ea:
13	1: 3⅞″	1:
14, 15	1 ea: H1	
16	1: A	
17	1: A	
18	1: 1½″	

DAISY, DAISY

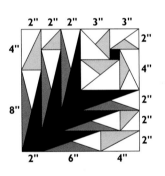

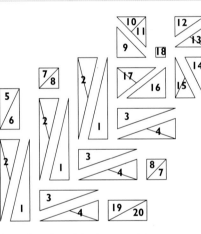

Templates: A, B, C, H1, K1
Color photo on page 16.

Note: *Sew the unit in the upper right corner of this block with a partial seam. See Partial Seam Construction (Chapter 1, page 11).*

PATCH	CUT	SUBCUT
1	3: C	
2	3: C	
3	3: B	
4	3: B	
5, 6	1 ea: A	
7, 8	1 ea: 2⅞″	2 ea:
9	1: 3⅞″	1:
10, 11	1 ea: 4¼″	1 ea:
12	1: H1	
13	1: H1	◁
14	1: A	
15	1: A	
16	1: K1	
17	1: K1	◁
18	1: 1½″	
19, 20	1 ea: A	

CRAB CAKES

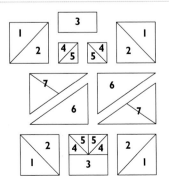

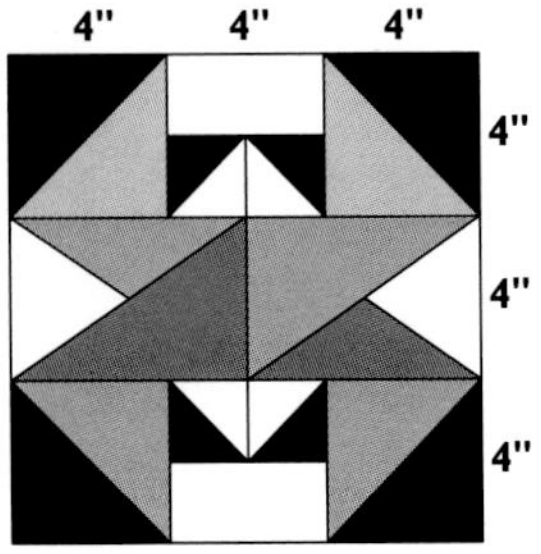

Template: H; Color photo on page 16.

PATCH	CUT	SUBCUT
1, 2	2 ea: 4⅞″	4 ea:
3	2: 2½″ x 4½″	
4, 5	2 ea: 2⅞″	4 ea:
6	2: H	
7	2: H	

HYDRANGEA

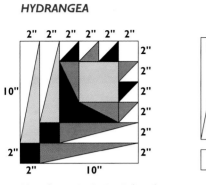

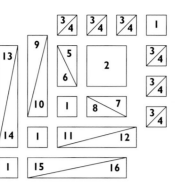

PATCH	CUT	SUBCUT
1	4: 2½"	
2	1: 4½"	
3, 4	3 ea: 2⅞"	6 ea:
5, 6	1 ea: A	
7, 8	1 ea: A	
9, 10	1 ea: C	
11, 12	1 ea: C	
13, 14	1 ea: D	
15, 16	1 ea: D	

Templates: A, C, D; Color photo on page 16.

PALM FROND

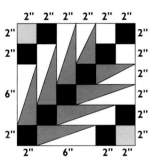

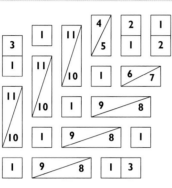

PATCH	CUT
1	10: 2½"
2	2: 2½"
3	2: 2½"
4, 5	1 ea: A
6, 7	1 ea: A
8, 9	3 ea: B
10, 11	3 ea: B

Templates: A, B; Color photo on page 16.

BEE'S KNEES

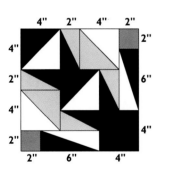

PATCH	CUT	SUBCUT
1, 2, 5, 6	1 ea: 4⅞"	2 ea:
3, 4	2 ea: A	
7	2: 2½"	
8, 9	2 ea: A	
10, 11	1 ea: B	
12, 13	1 ea: B	
14	1: 4½"	

Note: This block has areas that require partial seam construction. See Chapter 1, page 11.

Templates: A, B; Color photo on page 17.

BABY BIRDS

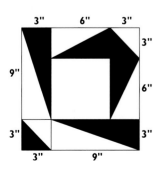

PATCH	CUT	SUBCUT
1, 2	1 ea: E	
3, 4	1 ea: 3⅞"	2 ea:
5, 6	1 ea: E	
7	1: 6½"	
8, 9	1 ea: G	
10, 11	1 ea: G	

Templates: E, G; Color photo on page 17.

AGATE PASS

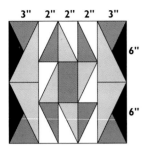

Templates: **A, E;** Color photo on page 17.

PATCH	CUT
1	2: E
2	2: E
3	2: E
4	2: E
5	1: $2\frac{1}{2}'' \times 4\frac{1}{2}''$
6–13	1 ea: A
14–21	1 ea: A

TAFFY PULL

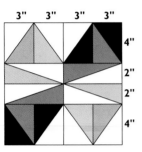

Templates: **B, K1;** Color photo on page 17.

PATCH	CUT
1–4	2 ea: K1
5–8	2 ea: K1
9, 10	2 ea: B
11, 12	2 ea: B

LIGHTNING BUG

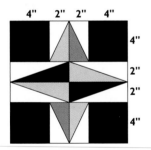

Templates: **A, B;** Color photo on page 17.

PATCH	CUT
1	4: $4\frac{1}{2}''$
2, 3	2 ea: B
4, 5	2 ea: B
6, 7	2 ea: A
8, 9	2 ea: A

TIGER EYE

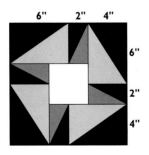

Templates: **A, H;** Color photo on page 17.

PATCH	CUT
1, 2	4 ea: H
3, 4	4 ea: A
5	1: $4\frac{1}{2}''$

Note: Sew this block together with a partial seam. See Partial Seam Construction (Chapter 1, page 11).

JOYFUL NOISE

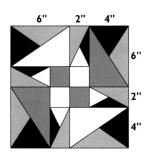

6" 2" 4"

6"
2"
4"

Templates: A, H; Color photo on page 17.

PATCH	CUT
1	4: H
2	4: H
3	4: A
4	4: A
5, 6	2 ea: 2½"

Note: Sew this block together with a partial seam. See Partial Seam Construction (Chapter 1, page 11).

FIRST STAR

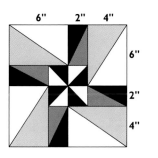

6" 2" 4"

6"
2"
4"

Templates: A, H; Color photo on page 17

PATCH	CUT	SUBCUT
1, 2	4 ea: H	
3, 4	4 ea: A	
5, 6	2 ea: 2⅞"	4 ea:

FOUR LEAF CLOVER

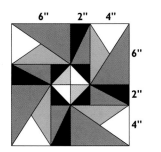

6" 2" 4"

6"
2"
4"

Templates: A, H; Color photo on page 17.

PATCH	CUT	SUBCUT
1	4: H	
2	4: H	
3, 4	4 ea: A	
5, 6	1 ea: 2⅞"	2 ea:
7, 8	1 ea: 2⅞"	2 ea:

ORANGEADE

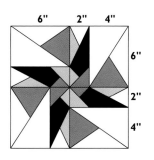

6" 2" 4"

6"
2"
4"

Templates: A, H; Color photo on page 17.

PATCH	CUT	SUBCUT
1	4: H	
2	4: H	
3	4: A	
4	4: A	
5, 6	1 ea: 3¼"	4 ea:
7	2: 2⅞"	4:

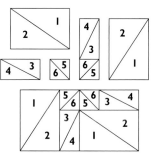
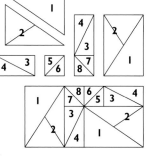
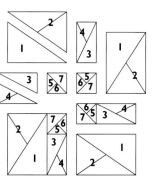

SHOOTING STAR

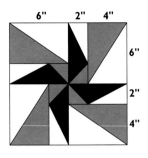

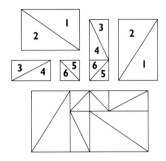

PATCH	CUT	SUBCUT
1, 2	4 ea: H	
3, 4	4 ea: A	
5, 6	2 ea: 2⁷⁄₈″	4 ea:

Templates: A, H; Color photo on page 17.

SALISBURY

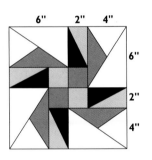

PATCH	CUT
1	4: H
2	4: H
3, 4	4 ea: A
5, 6	2 ea: 2½″

Template: A, H; Color photo on page 17.

HANCOCK

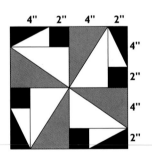

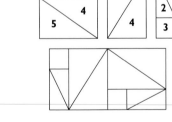

PATCH	CUT
1, 2	4 ea: A
3	4: 2½″
4, 5	4 ea: H

Templates: A, H; Color photo on page 18.

MAD HATTER

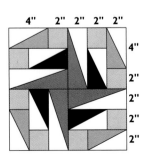

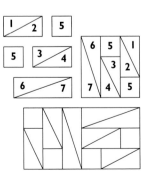

PATCH	CUT
1–4	4 ea: A
5	8: 2½″
6, 7	4 ea: B

Templates: A, B; Color photo on page 18.

KEEP RIGHT

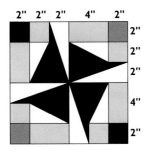

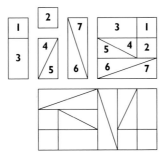

PATCH	CUT
1, 2	4 ea: 2½″
3	4: 2½″ x 4½″
4, 5	4 ea: A
6, 7	4 ea: B

Templates: A, B; Color photo on page 18.

PEMBROKE

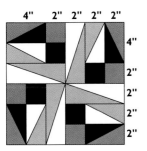

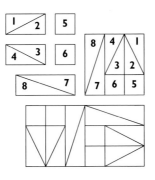

PATCH	CUT
1, 2	4 ea: A
3, 4	4 ea: A
5, 6	4 ea: 2½″
7, 8	4 ea: B

Templates: A, B; Color photo on page 18.

PARK PLACE

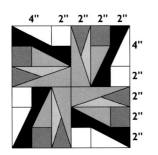

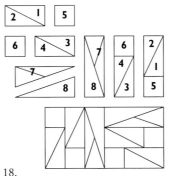

PATCH	CUT
1–4	4 ea: A
5, 6	4 ea: 2½″
7	4: B
8	4: B

Templates: A, B; Color photo on page 18.

NOONDAY SUN

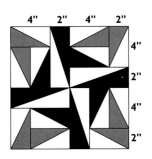

PATCH	CUT
1, 2	8 ea: A
3, 4	4 ea: A
5, 6	4 ea: B

Templates: A, B; Color photo on page 18.

HEADED HOME

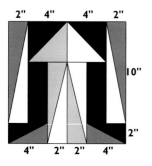

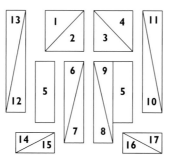

PATCH	CUT	SUBCUT
1–4	1 ea: 4⅞"	1 ea:
5	2: 2½" x 6½"	
6, 7	1 ea: C	
8, 9	1 ea: C	
10, 11	1 ea: D	
12, 13	1 ea: D	
14, 15	1 ea: A	
16, 17	1 ea: A	

Templates: A, C, D; Color photo on page 18.

HEART'S DESIRE

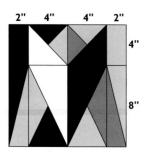

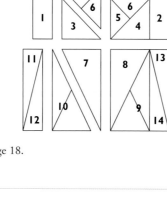

PATCH	CUT	SUBCUT
1, 2	1 ea: 2½" x 4½"	
3, 4	1 ea: 4⅞"	1 ea:
5, 6	1 ea: 5¼"	2 ea:
7	1: I	
8	1: I	
9	1: I	
10	1: I	
11, 12	1 ea: C	
13, 14	1 ea: C	

Templates: C, I; Color photo on page 18.

MARCH OF THE DIAMONDS

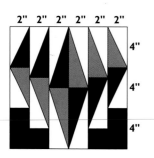

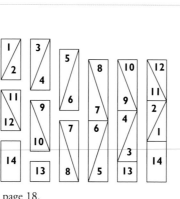

PATCH	CUT
1, 2	2 ea: A
3, 4	2 ea: J1
5, 6	2 ea: B
7, 8	2 ea: B
9, 10	2 ea: J1
11, 12	2 ea: A
13	2: 2½"
14	2: 2½" x 4½"

Templates: A, B, J1; Color photo on page 18.

ALL SHOOK UP

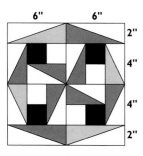

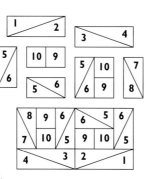

PATCH	CUT
1, 2	2 ea: B
3, 4	2 ea: B
5, 6	6 ea: A
7, 8	2 ea: A
9, 10	4 ea: 2½"

Templates: A, B; Color photo on page 19.

TILTED WINDMILL

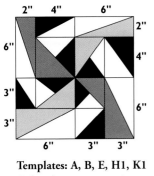

2" 4" 6"
6"
3"
3"
6" 3" 3"

2"
4"
6"

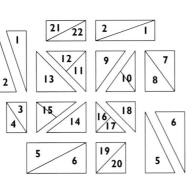

Templates: A, B, E, H1, K1
Color photo on page 19.

PATCH	CUT	SUBCUT
1, 2	2 ea: B	
3, 4	1 ea: H1	
5, 6	2 ea: E	
7, 8	1 ea: K1	
9	1: K1	
10	1: K1	
11, 12	1 ea: 5¼″	1 ea:
13	1: 4⅞″	1:
14	1: K1	
15	1: K1	
16, 17	1 ea: 4¼″	1 ea:
18–20	1 ea: 3⅞″	1 ea:
21, 22	1 ea: A	

SPIRAL STAIRCASE

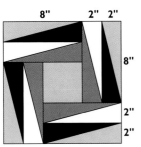

9" 3"
3"
6"
3"
9" 3"

3"
6"
6"

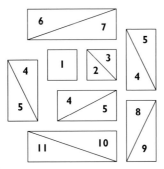

Templates: E, G; Color photo on page 19.

PATCH	CUT	SUBCUT
1	1: 3½″	
2, 3	1 ea: 3⅞″	1 ea:
4, 5	3 ea: E	
6, 7	1 ea: G	
8, 9	1 ea: E	
10, 11	1 ea: G	

TORNADO

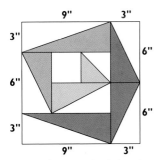

8" 2" 2"
8"
2"
2"

Template: C; Color photo on page 19.

PATCH	CUT
1–4	4 ea: C
5	1: 4½″

*Note: Sew this block together with a partial seam.
See Partial Seam Construction (Chapter 1, page 11).*

BRAIDED BOUNDS

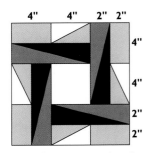

4" 4" 2" 2"
4"
4"
2"
2"

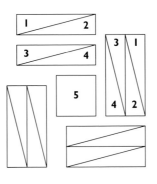

Templates: A, C; Color photo on page 19.

PATCH	CUT
1	4: 2½″ x 4½″
2, 3	4 ea: A
4, 5	4 ea: C
6	1: 4½″

*Note: Sew this block together with a partial seam. See
Partial Seam Construction (Chapter 1, page 11).*

SIESTA

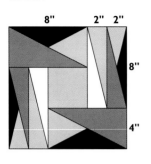

8" 2" 2"

8"

4"

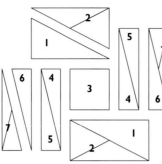

Templates: C, I; Color photo on page 19.

PATCH	CUT
1	2: I
2	2: I
3	1: 4½″
4–6	2 ea: C
7	2: C

Note: Sew this block together with a partial seam. See Partial Seam Construction (Chapter 1, page 11).

CAROUSEL

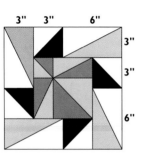

3" 3" 6"

3"

3"

6"

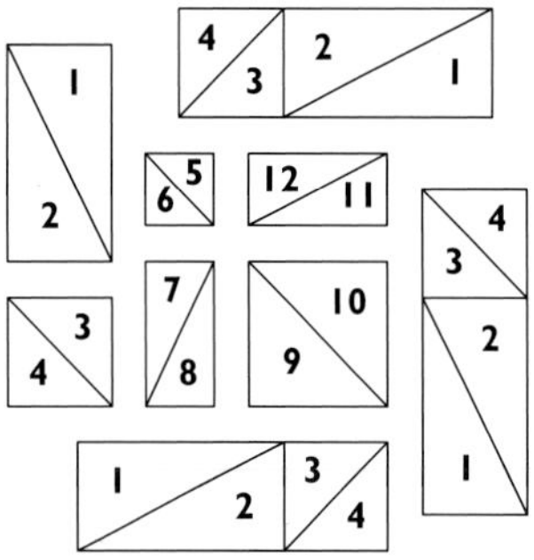

Templates: A, E; Color photo on page 19.

PATCH	CUT	SUBCUT
1, 2	4 ea: E	
3, 4	2 ea: 3⅞″	4 ea:
5, 6	1 ea: 2⅞″	1 ea:
7, 8	1 ea: A	
9, 10	1 ea: 4⅞″	1 ea:
11, 12	1 ea: A	

Note: Sew this block together with a partial seam. See Partial Seam Construction (Chapter 1, page 11).

MOONGLOW

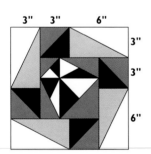

3" 3" 6"

3"

3"

6"

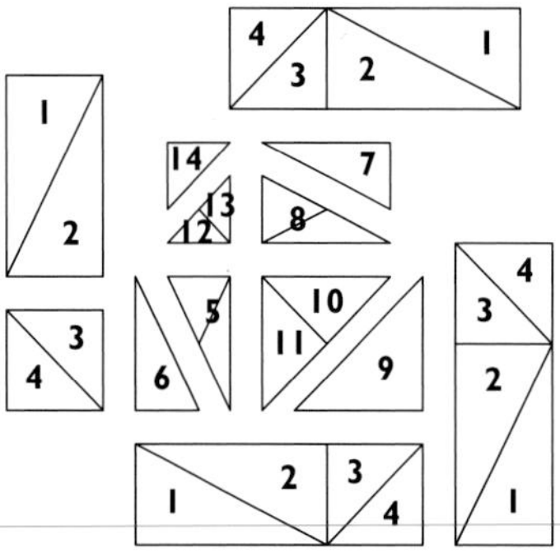

Templates: A, E
Color photo on page 19.

PATCH	CUT	SUBCUT
1, 2	4 ea: E	
3, 4	2 ea: 3⅞″	4 ea:
5	1: A	
6	1: A	
7	1: A	
8	1: A	
9	1: 4⅞″	1:
10, 11	1 ea: 5¼″	1 ea:
12, 13	1 ea: 3¼″	1 ea:
14	1: 2⅞″	1:

Note: Sew this block together with a partial seam. See Partial Seam Construction (Chapter 1, page 11).

CHUGGIN' ALONG

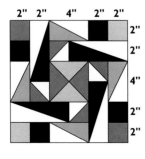

2" 2" 4" 2" 2"

2"

2"

4"

2"

2"

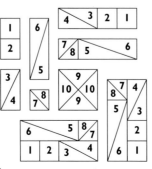

Templates: A, B; Color photo on page 19.

PATCH	CUT	SUBCUT
1, 2	4 ea: 2½″	
3, 4	4 ea: A	
5, 6	4 ea: B	
7, 8	2 ea: 2⅞″	4 ea:
9, 10	1 ea: 5¼″	2 ea:

Note: Sew this block together with a partial seam. See Partial Seam Construction (Chapter 1, page 11).

Block Variations

You can easily develop your own versions of the blocks presented in this chapter. To create them, make photocopies of the gray-scale drawings of a selected block, or trace the block outline and vary the placement of light, medium, and dark by shading or coloring the drawings.

You may also discover block variations during the sewing process. Cut out the pieces for a block and sew the triangles together. Play with the resulting squares and rectangles by rotating them to see what other effects you may get. Turn rectangles upside down; rotate pieced squares just a quarter turn to the right or to the left to create an entirely different block.

Here's another fun experiment. Make an assortment of various sizes of pieced squares and rectangles (each of which has only one diagonal seam). Assemble them as if they were a jigsaw puzzle on your design wall. Perhaps the result will be like the quilt *Starry Starry,* made by Beth Matsui Rice.

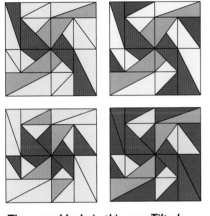

The same block, in this case Tilted Windmill (page 41), can look very different depending on the shading.

Another way to make variations is to take a very complex block and eliminate the seamlines. You can eliminate seamlines one by one and use different variations of the same block in a given quilt. For example, in my quilt *Coral Ribbons,* I used the following four versions of Buttercup Glory:

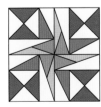
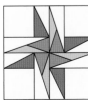

Buttercup Glory variations

■ *Starry Starry*
by Beth Matsui Rice, Catonsville, MD, 43″ × 48½″, 2004.

■ *Coral Ribbons*
by Margaret J. Miller, Bremerton, WA, 57″ × 57″, 2004. Quilted by Wanda Rains. Block used: variations of Buttercup Glory (page 22).

If you are making a block that has a direction to it, such as a pinwheel that spins to the right, you can easily create a second block in which it spins the opposite direction. To do this, cut the block pieces through four layers of two fabrics. Each fabric will have a right side up and a wrong side up. Sew all the right-side-up fabrics into one block; sew the wrong-side-up fabrics into a second block. Even such a small change can dramatically alter the look of a quilt.

Traditional blocks that have a significant number of diagonal lines are more interesting when skewed than those with only perpendicular lines. Patsi Hanseth used a traditional Ribbon Star block in her quilt *Marty Made Me Do It;* her distortion of the Nine-Patch grid makes the stars fairly dance across the surface.

The traditional block Card Trick lends itself well to this kind of distortion, since it contains a significant number of diagonal lines. The diagonal lines in a given patchwork pattern are what change angle, not the horizontal and vertical ones. Mabel Huseby, in her quilt *Distorted Deck,* makes it look like centrifugal force is spinning her distorted blocks away from the dignified traditional block in the center!

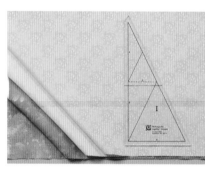

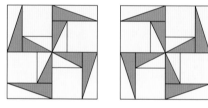

Reinterpreting traditional Nine-Patch blocks opens many doors to updating a quilt block design. Try your favorite Nine-Patch blocks in the following distorted, or skewed, grids.

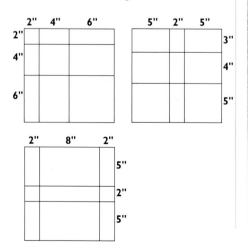

■ *Marty Made Me Do It* by Patsi Hanseth, Mount Vernon, WA, 35″ × 35″, 2004. Patsi reinterpreted the traditional Ribbon Star block with AnglePlay™ templates to create the skewed star blocks in this quilt.

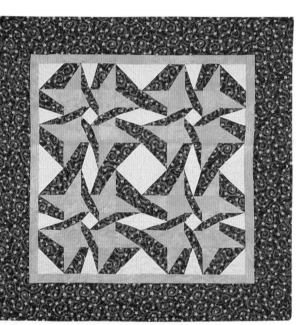

■ *Distorted Deck* by Mabel Huseby, Mount Vernon, WA, 60″ × 60″, 2004. Mabel made this quilt look like the Card Trick block on a rapidly spinning card table!

Margaret Fourhman's quilt *But It's a Dry Heat* also gives Card Trick a new look, using the first distortion shown in the illustration on page 44.

A good way to become familiar with the magic of this half-rectangle shape is to make a number of blocks that are unrelated in design. Choose a dozen blocks from the previous pages that

strike your fancy. Cut and stitch them to see what kind of quilt develops! The blocks can be stark and crisp, as in Nancy Anderson's *AnglePlay Sampler*. Note that Nancy chose some blocks that are "contained," while others seem to want to whirl out beyond their borders.

Although Beth Gardner has many of the same blocks in her sampler quilt *Intermezzo Unexpected,* the blocks are much more subtle when interpreted with hand-dyed fabrics. They appear to float gently on the surface of this quilt.

My quilt *Batiks, Etc.* (cover and title page) shows that you don't need many sampler blocks to make an interesting wall quilt. The offset arrangement of these blocks, plus the fact that they come out and invade the border in several places, keep this from looking like a predictable sampler quilt.

More ideas for innovative ways of assembling blocks into a quilt can be found in Chapter 4, as well as in my book *Smashing Sets: Innovative Settings for Traditional Quilt Blocks*. The most important thing though, is to have fun playing!

BLOCKS TO QUILTS

I f you would like to play with design, photocopy the pages on which your shaded blocks appear, and play with arrangements of them on a sheet of graph paper.

Perhaps the simplest approach is to choose a simple block and repeat it side-by-side in the quilt. Sometimes the block lends itself to the formation of a tessellated design. Both quilts below were made from the same quilt block, Periscope (page 22), but different coloration produced very different results.

In Teri Bever's quilt *Red Sky at Night…*, it is hard to tell where one block stops and the next one begins. Surely, quilt show viewers will pause by this one to figure out what Teri did to get the stars so close together and touching with such sharp points!

Though Janet Lane-Tranbarger used the same Periscope block, her quilt looks like interlocking puzzle pieces.

Another approach is to combine two blocks checkerboard-style in the quilt. Choose blocks that blend in such a way that the design from one really reaches into the neighboring block. A block with a strong X feeling to it, next to a self-contained block would do the trick. A couple examples appear here.

Blocks used: variation of Tilted Windmill (page 41), Twisted (page 24), variation of Moonglow (page 42).

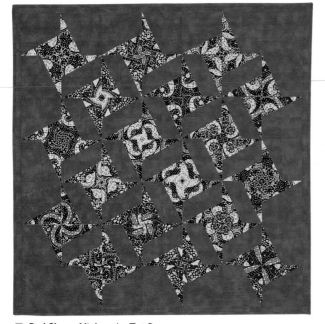

■ *Red Sky at Night…* by Teri Bever, Sedro Woolley, WA, 43″ × 43″, 2004. Block used: Periscope (page 22).

■ *Untitled* by Janet Lane-Tranbarger, Riverside, CA, 32″ × 32″, 2004. Block used: Periscope (page 22).

Play with a very graphic block and make "positive" and "negative" versions of it. Two versions of a strong block in a quilt could be striking.

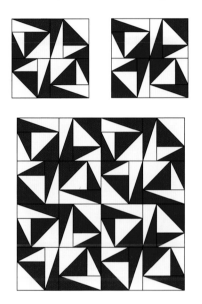

Try offsetting the blocks. This can be done by offsetting a portion of the block (half-block, quarter-block, etc.) or by matching up seamlines so that a shape in one block reaches into the neighboring block. My quilts *Coral Ribbons* (page 43) and *Raspberry Parfait* below are examples of this.

Note that when you offset blocks, as shown in the illustration at right, there is an empty space between the edges of the blocks. You may choose to fill that with a single fabric or perhaps a simplified patchwork element from the blocks that are offset. In the case of *Raspberry Parfait*, I had a 9″ "hole" to fill, so I made a number of the 6″ block centers from the original pattern, added 2″ border strips, then trimmed to a 9½″ square to fill between the original blocks.

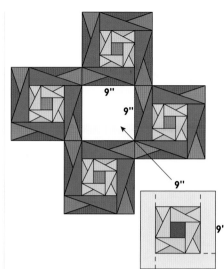

In Patsi Hanseth's *Untitled* quilt, she built on the whirling feeling of the Polliwog block (page 29) by filling in with a patchwork pinwheel that seems to spin in the opposite direction. Note the optical illusion Patsi has created—when you look once, you think the mauve shapes are the center of the main block of the quilt; if you blink and look again, the print pinwheels seem to be the center of the theme block!

■ *Raspberry Parfait* by Margaret J. Miller, Bremerton, WA, 53″ × 53″, 2004. Machine quilted by Wanda Rains. Block used: Spiderweb (page 28).

■ *Untitled* by Patsi Hanseth, Mount Vernon, WA, 42″ × 56″, 2004. Block used: Polliwog (page 29).

Try overlapping a corner patch. Again, there will be an empty space between blocks (shown below in bright yellow). However, this space is easily filled by making either a block of a different design or a traditional filler, such as a checkerboard, . . . quarter-square triangles, a square of interesting fabric, and so on.

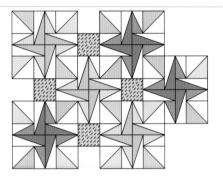

Andrea Rudman did some block overlapping in her quilt *It's Not Blue*. Note that her blocks seem to overlap two shapes in a neighboring block, making it appear that the yellow blocks are superimposed on the coral ones. This is another AnglePlay variation of the traditional Card Trick block!

Any of these approaches camouflages where one block stops and its neighbor begins. They produce a quilt that is not only more interesting to piece but also more interesting to look at!

If the block is a four-patch block, play with rotating the four quarters before you sew it together. All the blocks in my quilt *Rainbow Ribbons* (opposite page) are made with the same four-

patch unit, rotated and created with slightly different fabric combinations.

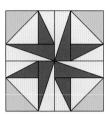
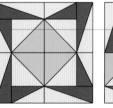
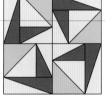
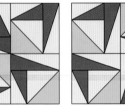
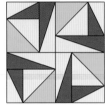

■ *It's Not Blue* by Andrea Rudman, Kingston, WA, 48″ × 48″, 2004. Block used: variation of traditional block Doris's Delight.

Rainbow Ribbons by Margaret J. Miller, Bremerton, WA, 68″ × 68″, 2004. Machine quilted by Wanda Rains. Blocks used: Variation of Janet's Fancy (page 21), with four-patches rotated.

Sunflower by Margaret J. Miller, Bremerton, WA, 71″ × 71″, 2004. Machine quilted by Wanda Rains. Blocks used: Hide and Seek (page 32), Leaves of Grass (page 33), Morning Glory (page 34).

My favorite blocks to work with are the directional (asymmetrical) ones. Many more options for interesting quilt design are present when rotating either a single block or a group of directional blocks. Note that in my quilt *Sunflower,* there are only three different blocks in the quilt; but since all three are directional blocks, they make a strong graphic design. Imagine how different the center of this quilt would look with different orientations of the Sunflower blocks. Note also the framing border formed by the green shapes at the edges of the Hide and Seek blocks (page 32) in the corners of the quilt.

Connie Tiegel also used a number of directional blocks in her quilt *Bloomin' of the Rose*. Note the gentle whirling of the four Baby Birds blocks (page 35) and how they draw the action out of the center of this quilt, which is four subtly colored Bee's Knees blocks (page 35).

The blocks in this book are dramatic as straight blocks because of the variety of angles the AnglePlay™ templates afford. But looking at all these blocks on-point reveals another world of possibilities. Dixie McClain made two quilts using the same block—Scout's Star (page 24). In the first quilt, *Come Play With Me,* note how her use of value made some stars stand out and others fade into the background.

■ *Bloomin' of the Rose* by Connie Tiegel, Atherton, CA, 48″ × 48″, 2004. Hand quilted by Deb Walsh.
Blocks used: Bee's Knees (page 35), Baby Birds (page 35), variation of Spiderweb (page 28).

■ *Come Play With Me* by Dixie McClain, Eden, ID, 58″ × 58″, 2004. Machine quilted by Ann Trotter.
Block used: Scout's Star (page 24).

In her second quilt, using the same block but on-point, Dixie created an entirely new look. By using plaids and light fabrics in a very dramatic way, the stars seem crisp and brilliant. Note how she used a partial block as filler triangles at the edge of the quilt, which look like birds flying around the edge.

The half-rectangle triangle creates lots of visual excitement in a pieced quilt because of the numerous angles that can be incorporated into the patchwork. You will find that you don't need a complicated block to create an intriguing quilt; the change in the diagonal seam's angle creates design that flows across your quilt surface. You may also have discovered by now that half-rectangle triangles would be too sharp or angry looking if used exclusively; it's the combination of this new shape with traditional squares and half-square triangles that breathes new life into patchwork design.

■ *Why Not Plaids and Stripes?* by Dixie McClain, Eden, ID, 60″ × 60″, 2004. Machine quilted by Ann Trotter. Block used: Scout's Star (page 24).

GALLERY
OF QUILTS

The photos in this chapter should put yet another perspective on the blocks presented thus far. Each of these quilts was made by someone who either took the AnglePlay workshop or participated in early experimental classes. The latter students were given a selected assortment of the blocks shown in Chapter 3 (pages 20–45) and only basic guidelines as to how to create a quilt with them.

In the caption with each photograph, you will see not only the name of the quiltmaker but also, where appropriate, the name and location of the blocks used in her quilt.

This is just a glimpse of the possibilities attainable with the AnglePlay shape. For those who love traditional piecing, incorporating this new shape into the nine-patch, four-patch, and other blocks we have loved through the years will surely transform the pieced quilts of the 21st century. Have fun with it!

■ *Heliconia* by Marilyn Hiestand, Hawaii National Park, HI, 60″ × 90″, 2004. Blocks used: Canasta (page 32), Palm Frond (page 35), Baby Birds (page 35), variation of Deal 'Em Out (page 21).

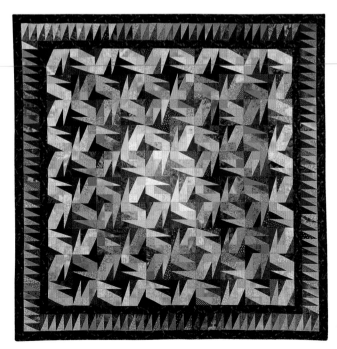

■ *Is It Purple or Orange?* by Pamela Thomas, Hayward, CA, 76″ × 76″, 2004. Block used: Reverse version of the Mad Hatter block (page 38).

■ *A Deep Sea Adventure with
Margaret J. Miller* by Shelby Boyd,
Franklin, TN, 42 × 42″, 2004.
Block used: Lightning Bug (page 36).

■ *Cartwheel* by Cathy Hamilton,
Arcata, CA, 48″ × 48″, 2004.
Block used: Variation of Ann's
Plans (page 24).

■ *Ferns* by Connie Tiegel,
Atherton, CA, 48″ × 48″, 2004.
Block used: Canasta (page 32).

■ *Carnival* by Patsi Hanseth,
Mount Vernon, WA, 35″ × 47″, 2004.
Block used: Four-patch variation of
the North Star block (page 25).

■ *Night Music* by Karen Fettig Abramson,
Poughkeepsie, NY, 54″ × 45″, 2004. Block centers
by Barbara Powers, Yorktown Heights, NY.
Machine quilted by Karen Fettig Abramson.
Block used: variation of Spiderweb (page 28). It has
2″ rather than 3″ units along the edges.

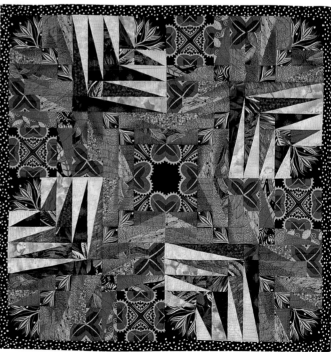

■ *Hot Tropics* by Jan Brown,
Trinidad, CA, 42″ × 42″, 2004.
Machine quilted by Angela McMahon.
Block used: variation of Folded Fern
(page 31).

■ *Open Windows* by Reynola Pakusich, Bellingham,
WA, 42″ × 62″, 2004. Outer units are 2″ square and
2″ × 4″, instead of 3″ square and 3″ × 6″, with 4″
half-square triangles in the corner.

■ *Sarah Likes Pink, I Think* by
Cathy C. Bertrand, Nashville, TN,
52″ × 52″, 2004.
Block used: Palm Frond (page 35).

■ *When the Threads of Marriage Begin
to Unravel* by Elise Fare, Jacksonville, FL,
30″ × 30″, 2004.
Blocks used: Barbed Wire (page 22),
Buttercup Glory (page 22), and Pretty
Posey (page 33).

Season's Greetings by Kathy Geehan, Bainbridge Island, WA, 52″ × 72″, 2003. Machine quilted by Wanda Rains. Outer units are 2″ square and 2″ × 4″, instead of 3″ square and 3″ × 6″, around 4″ finished conversation-print centers.

Untitled by Faye Nutting, Sitka, AK, 33″ × 39″, 2004. Block used: Twist Tie (page 29).

Purple Stars for Rachel by Cathy C. Bertrand, Nashville, TN, 52″ × 52″, 2004. Block used: Christmas Star (page 21).

The Pansy Way Out by Kendra Allen,
Poulsbo, WA, 36″ × 36″, 2001.
Block used: variation of Spiderweb (page 28).

Dyslexic Baby Quilt by Margaret J.
Miller, Bremerton, WA, 43″ × 50″, 2004.
Machine quilted by Jennifer Pielow.
Block used: variation of Spiderweb
(page 28). Outer units are 2″ × 8″
instead of 3″ × 9″; centers are 2½″
finished squares with 1″ × 2½″
sashing strips.

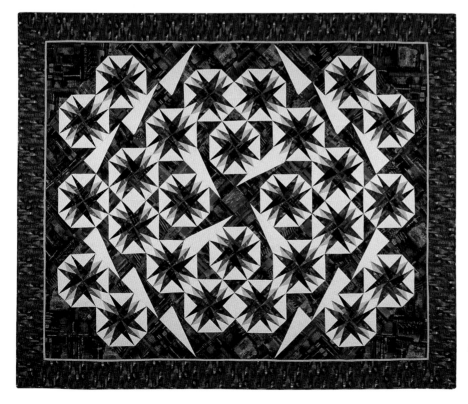

Color Me Bright by Maurine Roy,
Edmonds, WA, 81″ × 97″, 2004.
Block used: Christmas Star (page 21)

A
TEMPLATE PATTERNS

This section includes drawings of the AnglePlay™ template shapes used in this book. Trace these shapes onto heavy template plastic. Since you will be tracing around this template onto fabric, a flimsy template plastic just won't do. Make your tracings carefully with a fine-tip felt pen, and cut them out carefully.

On each template, the numbers near the base of the triangle are the finished size of the larger triangle; the upper numbers are the finished size of the half-size triangle. Don't forget to trace the half-diagonal lines!

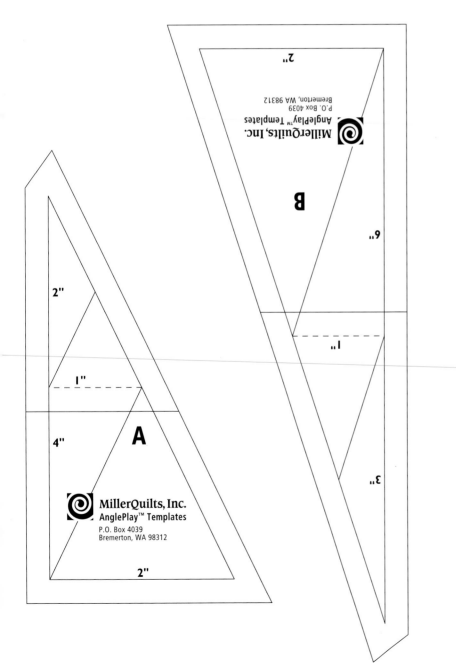

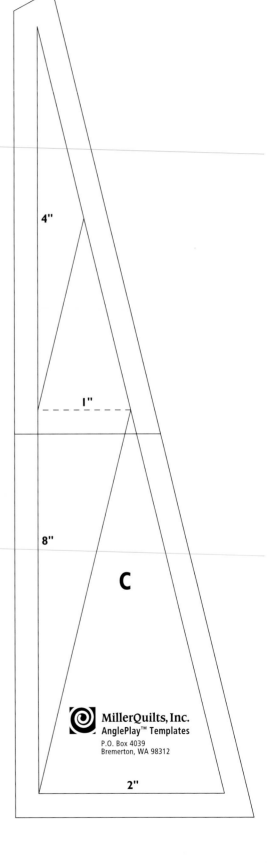

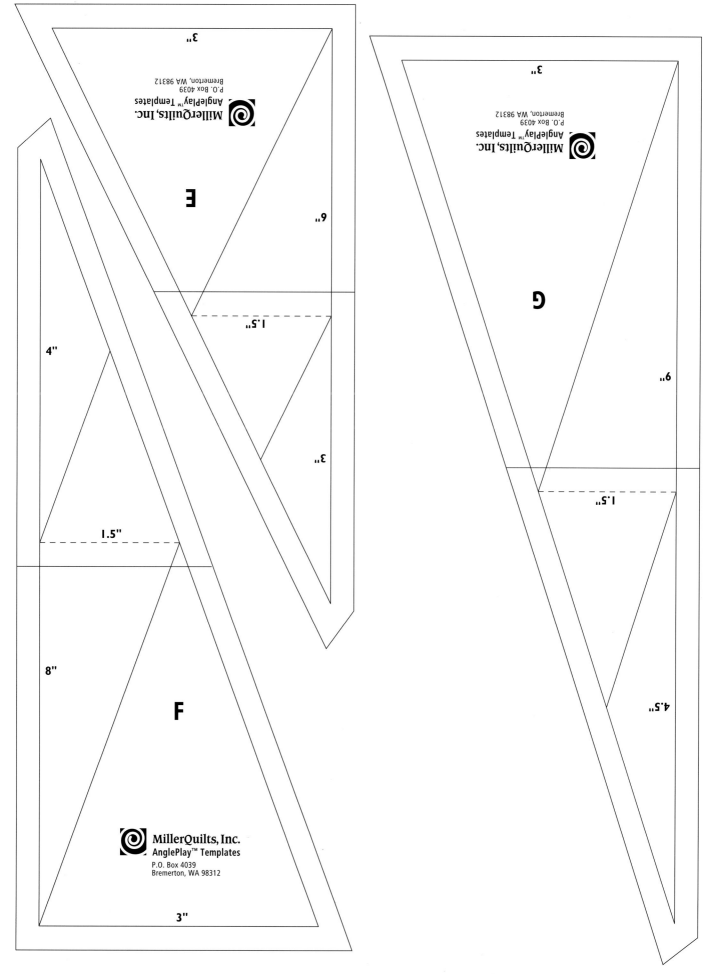

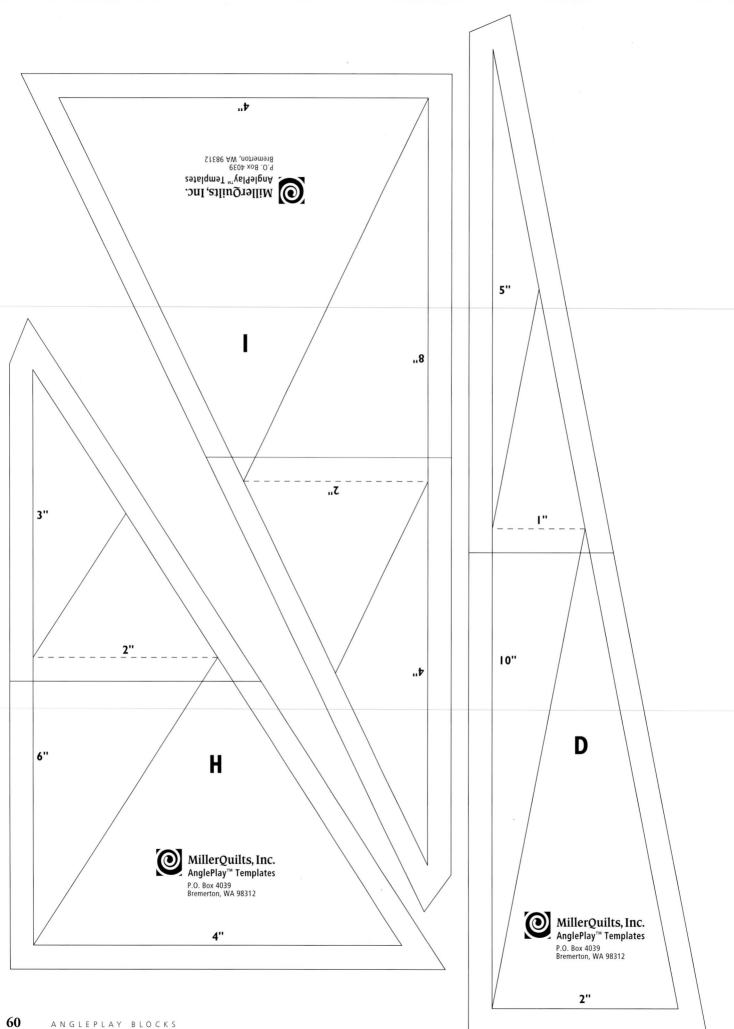

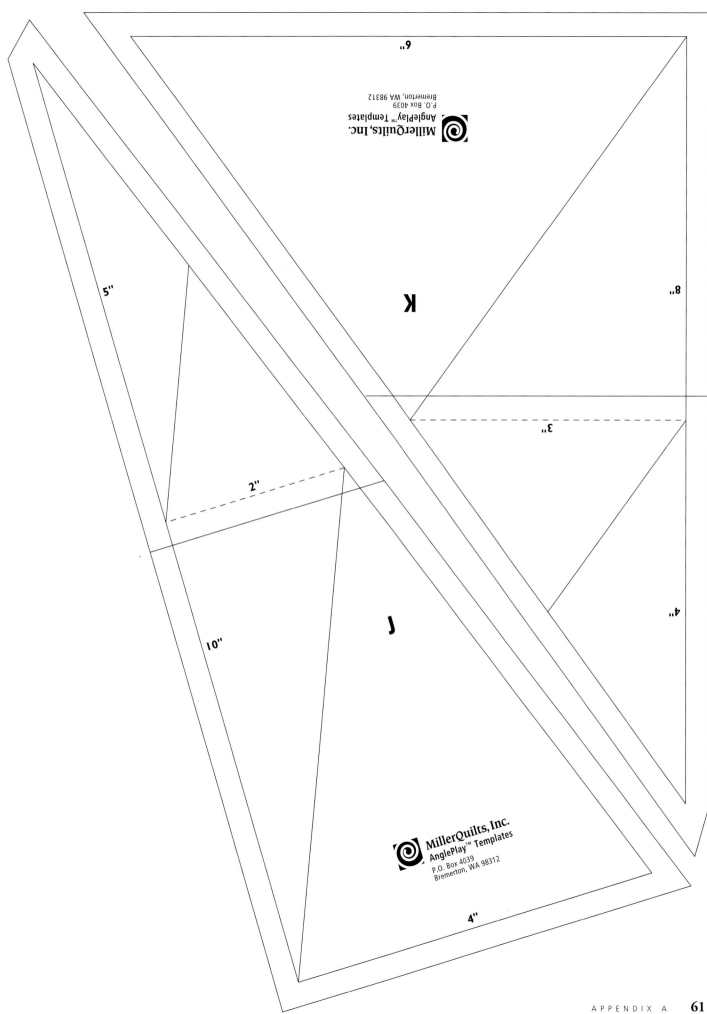

6"

MillerQuilts, Inc.
AnglePlay™ Templates
P.O. Box 4039
Bremerton, WA 98312

K

8"

5"

3"

2"

4"

10"

J

MillerQuilts, Inc.
AnglePlay™ Templates
P.O. Box 4039
Bremerton, WA 98312

4"

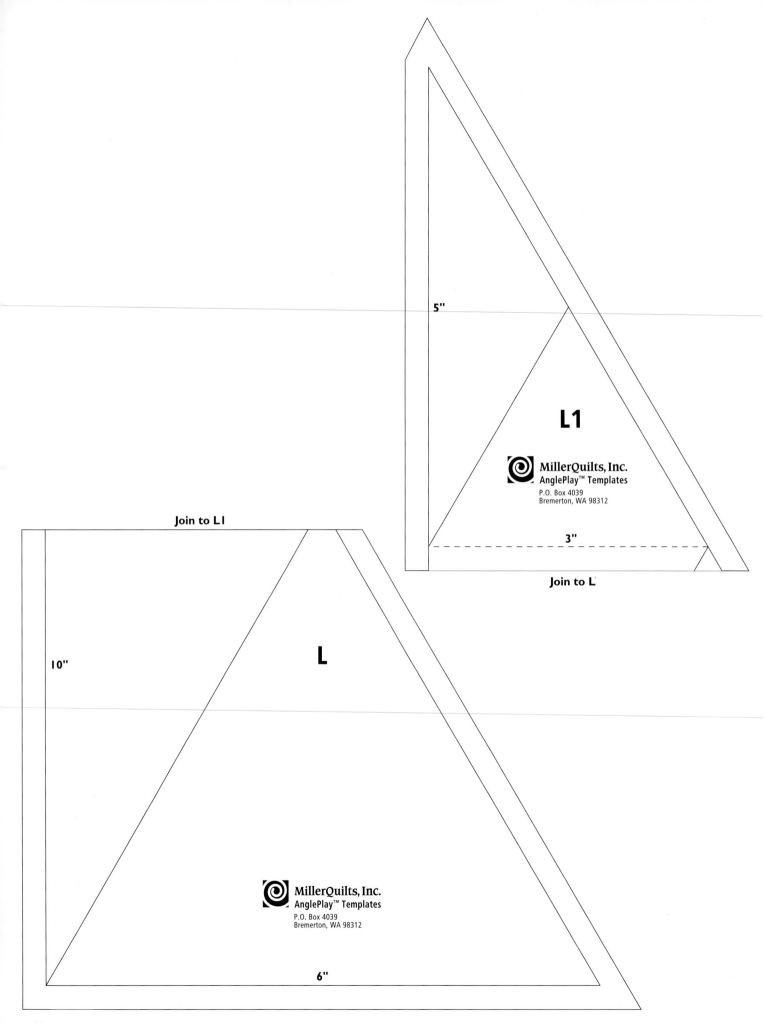

5"

L1

MillerQuilts, Inc.
AnglePlay™ Templates
P.O. Box 4039
Bremerton, WA 98312

3"

Join to L

Join to L1

10"

L

MillerQuilts, Inc.
AnglePlay™ Templates
P.O. Box 4039
Bremerton, WA 98312

6"

BLOCK INDEX

Note: *The first page reference is to the color photo of the block; the second page is the gray-scale diagram with cutting and piecing instructions.*

ABOUT THE AUTHOR

Margaret J. Miller is a studio quiltmaker who travels widely, giving lectures and workshops on color and design that encourage students to reach for the unexpected in contemporary and traditional quiltmaking. Her full teaching schedule has taken her throughout the United States and to many countries she would never have visited if it hadn't been for quiltmaking! Her presentations are known for their enthusiasm, humor, and sincere encouragement of quiltmakers at all levels of skill and experience.

Having done various forms of needlework throughout her life, Margaret learned to quilt and appliqué in 1978. At that time, she was on the textiles and clothing faculty of the home economics department at California Polytechnic State University, San Luis Obispo. One class she taught there, Creative Textiles, introduced her to the quiltmaking industry. She later moved to San Diego, where she joined her first quilt guild and started Tanglethread Junction, an appliqué and stained glass appliqué pattern business. She sold her business in 1982, as part of her commitment to becoming a full-time quiltmaker.

She currently makes her home in her beloved Pacific Northwest, an hour's ferry ride west of Seattle on the Kitsap Peninsula. There, her full life as a studio quiltmaker is punctuated by the squawking of crows and the call of seagulls. With the able advice and assistance of her studio cat, Patches, she creates quilted works for commissions, as well as for books and gallery shows. Many a day winds down with quiet time on the front deck, watching spectacular sunsets over the Olympic Mountains.

RESOURCES

COMPUTER QUILT PROGRAMS

Electric Quilt Company
419 Gould Street, Suite 2
Bowling Green, OH 43402
(800) 356-4219
www.electricquilt.com

Almost all the block designs were developed using the Electric Quilt 5 (EQ5) program. The work of designing, shading, and organizing the blocks went from overwhelming to doable thanks to this program!

CUTTING TOOLS

AnglePlay™ Templates
Available from MillerQuilts, Inc.
P.O. Box 4039
Bremerton, WA 98312
www.millerquilts.com

These templates are indispensable for rotary cutting the half-rectangle shape. Each template has its elongated tip trimmed at just the right angle to ensure perfect piecing results, taking all the guesswork out of how to match up two fabric triangles before sewing.

AnglePlay Caddy for AnglePlay™ Templates
Available from MillerQuilts, Inc.
P.O. Box 4039
Bremerton, WA 98312
www.millerquilts.com

The slotted rack keeps the templates at your fingertips and keeps the templates from getting lost on your worktable.

Rulersmith, Inc.
Makers of Omnigrid® and Omnigrip™ products
1560 Port Drive
Burlington, WA 98233
(360) 707-2828
www.rulersmith.com

All cutting products from this company are of the highest quality and accuracy. They are available at most quilt shops, fabric stores, and quilting supply catalogs.

MACHINE QUILTERS

Patsi Hanseth
21106 Mann Road
Mount Vernon, WA 98273
(360) 445-3575

Jennifer Pielow
6963 Barnard Way
Bremerton, WA 98312
(360) 308-9004 or (360) 620-3239
www.sewtimely.com

Wanda Rains
Rainy Day Quilts
22448 NE Jefferson Point Road
Kingston, WA 98346
(360) 297-5115
www.rainydayquilts.com

QUILT PHOTOGRAPHY

Mark Frey
P.O. Box 1596
Yelm, WA 98597
(360) 894-3591
E-mail:markfreyphoto@ywave.com

LECTURES & WORKSHOPS

For more information on lectures and workshops by Margaret J. Miller, write to her at P.O. Box 4039, Bremerton, WA 98312. Current teaching schedule and lecture/workshop topics are available at www.millerquilts.com.

BOOKS

Brackman, Barbara. *An Encyclopedia of Pieced Quilt Patterns.* Prairie Flower Publishing: Lawrence, KS, 1984.

Miller, Margaret J. *Smashing Sets: Innovative Settings for Sampler Blocks.* C&T Publishing: Concord, CA, 2000.